Alexander Peter Saccaro

380 Kurztests
die wirklich helfen
Englisch 5/6

Klett Lerntraining

Alexander P. Saccaro, Gymnasiallehrer für Englisch und Französisch, ist langjähriger Autor von Lehrwerken und Lernhilfen.

Bibliografische Information der Deutschen Bibliothek
Die Deutsche Bibliothek verzeichnet diese Publikation in der Deutschen Nationalbibliografie; detaillierte bibliografische Daten sind im Internet über http://dnb.ddb.de abrufbar.

Auflage 4. 3. 2. | 2015 2014 2013
Die letzten Zahlen bezeichnen jeweils die Auflage und das Jahr des Druckes.
Dieses Werk folgt der neuesten Rechtschreibung und Zeichensetzung. Ausnahmen bilden Texte, bei denen künstlerische, philologische oder lizenzrechtliche oder andere Gründe einer Änderung entgegenstehen.

www.klett.de/lernhilfen
Produktsteuerung: Sandra Meyer
Redaktion: Quaide N. Williams, Sandra Meyer
Satz: DTP-studio Andrea Eckhardt, Göppingen
Druck: Medienhaus Plump, Rheinbreitbach
Printed in Germany
ISBN 978-3-12-927254-1

9 783129 272541

Hallo liebe Schülerin, hallo lieber Schüler!

In diesem Buch findest du 380 Kurztests, mit denen du in Englisch jeden Tag ein bisschen besser werden kannst. Es bringt viel mehr, täglich in kleinen Portionen zu lernen, als kurz vor Klassenarbeiten oder Tests in einer Hauruck-Aktion.

Wieso 380 Kurztests?
Weil ein Schuljahr in der Regel 190 Schultage hat und in diesem Buch die wichtigsten Themen aus 2 Schuljahren zusammengestellt sind. Wenn du also an jedem Schultag einen Kurztest löst, kannst du ohne Stress besser werden.

Nimm dir täglich 10–15 Minuten Zeit!
Wenn du jeden Tag einen Kurztest machst, wird dir das wirklich helfen. Such dir eine Übung zu einem Thema aus, das dich am meisten interessiert oder das du gerade in der Schule durchnimmst. Nimm dir dann für das Lösen ca. 10 bis 15 Minuten Zeit.

So gehst du mit diesem Buch um:

1. Im Inhaltsverzeichnis sind **alle wichtigen Themen des 5. und 6. Schuljahrs** übersichtlich aufgelistet. Im Buch selbst findest du die Themen immer in den farbigen Balken am oberen Seitenrand.
2. Alle Kurztests sind in **3 Schwierigkeitsstufen** eingeteilt. An den 3 Sternen erkennst du, ob ein Kurztest leicht ★☆☆, mittelschwierig ★★☆ oder schwierig ★★★ ist.
3. Anhand der **ausführlichen Lösungen** kannst du überprüfen, ob du alles richtig gemacht hast. Die Lösungen zu jedem Kurztest stehen auf dem Kopf unten auf jeder Seite.
4. **Tipps** (wie z. B. bei Kurztest 53) helfen dir bei besonders kniffligen Aufgaben auf die Sprünge.
5. Dieses Buch ist so aufgebaut, dass du dir einzelne Kurztests zu bestimmten Themen aussuchen kannst. Du musst das Buch nicht von vorne nach hinten durcharbeiten.

Die Klett Lerntraining-Redaktion wünscht dir viel Erfolg!

1 ★☆☆ Regelmäßige Pluralbildung

Bilde den Plural der folgenden Substantive.

book ______	plan ______
plane ______	minute ______
answer ______	apple ______
face ______	chair ______
box ______	dress ______
table ______	page ______
sandwich ______	pencil case ______
bridge ______	desk ______
hour ______	brush ______
teacher ______	pupil ______

2 ★☆☆ Beachte die Aussprache!

Bei welchen der folgenden Substantive wird die Pluralendung wie /iz/ ausgesprochen? Unterstreiche diese Substantive.

pages	exercises	churches	clothes	houses
faces	roles	stages	theatres	buses
titles	languages	phrases	pieces	centres
bridges	cornflakes	messages	places	brochures
voices	noises	noses	horses	scenes
brushes	cakes	classes	glasses	tables

1 books, planes, answers, faces, boxes, tables, sandwiches, bridges, hours, teachers, plans, minutes, apples, chairs, dresses, pages, pencil cases, desks, brushes, pupils
2 pages, exercises, churches, clothes, houses, faces, roles, stages, theatres, buses, titles, languages, phrases, pieces, centres, bridges, cornflakes, messages, places, brochures, voices, noises, noses, horses, scenes, brushes, cakes, classes, glasses, tables

3 ★★☆ Und wie steht es mit dem Singular?

Bilde den Singular der folgenden Substantive.

days ____________________ boys ____________________

babies ____________________ families ____________________

thieves ____________________ plays ____________________

wives ____________________ knives ____________________

shelves ____________________ countries ____________________

parties ____________________ lives ____________________

halves ____________________ hobbies ____________________

4 ★★☆ Und noch einmal zum Plural

Setze die folgenden Substantive in den Plural.

a boy and a girl ____________________

a brother and a sister ____________________

a book on a shelf ____________________

a pupil and a teacher ____________________

a cat and a dog ____________________

a short life ____________________

a baby and a toy ____________________

a night and a day ____________________

a diary and a pen ____________________

a house and a flat ____________________

a bus and a lorry* ____________________

* lorry = LKW (American English: truck = trucks)

3 day, baby, thief, wife, shelf, party, half; boy, family, play, knife, country, life, hobby
4 boys and girls, brothers and sisters, books on shelves, pupils and teachers, cats and dogs, short lives, babies and toys, nights and days, diaries and pens, houses and flats, buses and lorries

5 ★★☆ Substantive mit unregelmäßigem Plural

Wie lautet der Plural?

man ____________________ woman ____________________

child ____________________ tooth ____________________

foot ____________________ goose ____________________

mouse ____________________

6 ★★☆ Und wie sieht es hier aus?

Bilde den Plural der folgenden Substantive.

a lady and a gentleman ____________________

a woman and a child ____________________

a bad tooth ____________________

the foot of a man ____________________

a cat and a mouse ____________________

7 ★★☆ Achte auf die richtige Schreibweise

Ergänze die fehlenden Buchstaben.

You can stand on one f ____________________.

What you eat, is your f ____________________.

For most people the first meal in the morning is b ____________________.

Your father and mother are your p ____________________.

Father, mother and children are a f ____________________.

The people who live next door are your n ____________________.

5 men, women, children, teeth, feet, geese, mice
6 ladies and gentlemen, women and children, bad teeth, the feet of men, cats and mice
7 foot, food, breakfast, parents, family, neighbours

8 ★★☆ Besonderheiten

Einige der folgenden Substantive sehen wie Singulare, andere wie Plurale aus. Wie musst du sie gebrauchen? Trage die folgenden Substantive bitte in die entsprechenden Rubriken ein.

news	information	people
mathematics	police	homework

nur im Singular	nur im Plural
news	mathematics
information	
police, homework	
people	

9 ★★★ Was ist richtig?

Vervollständige die Sätze, indem du die richtige Form von *to be* einträgst.

a) There _are_ too much homework. We really can't do it.

b) There are some people who think that homework _is_ fun.

c) These people _are_ completely wrong, I can tell you.

d) What's the homework for today? Well, there _is_ some maths homework, and there _is_ homework in English, German and Biology.

e) That _are_ bad news again. But thanks for the information though* it _is_ not very good.

* though = obwohl

8 Nur im Singular werden gebraucht: *news, mathematics, information, homework*. Als Plurale werden im Englischen immer *police* und *people* (= Leute, Menschen) gebraucht. Mit einem Plural-s bedeutet *peoples* im übrigen „Völker".
9 a) There is too much homework … **b)** … who think that homework is fun. **c)** These people are completely wrong … **d)** … there is some maths homework, and there is homework in … **e)** That is bad news again. But thanks for the information though it is not very good.

10 ★☆☆ Pluralwörter

Welche der folgenden Substantive kannst du nur im Plural gebrauchen?

glasses	socks	shoes	trousers	jeans
skirts	pyjamas	shorts	boots	shirts

Nur als Pluralform

____

____

11 ★★☆ Debbies Kleider

Debbies Schrank ist voller Kleider. Setze *a pair of, two pairs of …* ein, wo dies sinnvoll ist.

4 jeans	3 trousers	5 pyjamas
1 shorts	1 sunglasses	3 blouses
5 shoes	2 skirts	5 pullovers
7 socks	3 boots	1 coat

Debbie has got a lot of cothes. She has got

____

____

____

____

____

10 Nur als Pluralform möglich sind *glasses, trousers, jeans, pyjamas, shorts.*
11 She has got four pairs of jeans, three pairs of trousers, five pairs of pyjamas, a pair of shorts, a pair of sunglasses, three blouses, five pairs of shoes, two skirts, five pullovers, seven pairs of socks, three pairs of boots and one coat.

12 ★☆☆ Wer hat was und was gehört zu wem?

Verbinde die Substantive mit dem *s*-Genitiv.

Tom / house ______________________

Mr Benson / car ______________________

Mr Benson / wife ______________________

the Bensons / hobbies ______________________

my parents / bikes ______________________

my sisters / friends ______________________

my mother / brother ______________________

my brother / CDs ______________________

Mr Mason / lessons ______________________

the pupils / workbooks ______________________

my grandparents / radio ______________________

13 ★★☆ Der Plural des *s*-Genitivs

Setze die markierten Substantive in den Plural und verbinde sie mit dem *s*-Genitiv.

the baby / toys ______________________

the girl / mother ______________________

the boy / shoes ______________________

my uncle / brothers ______________________

my cousin / teacher ______________________

my aunt / letters ______________________

12 Tom's house, Mr Benson's car, Mr Benson's wife, the Bensons' hobbies, my parents' bikes, my sisters' friends, my mother's brother, my brother's CDs, Mr Mason's lessons, the pupils' workbooks, my grandparents' radio
13 the babies' toys, the girls' mother, the boys' shoes, my uncles' brothers, my cousins' teacher, my aunts' letters

14 ★★☆ Und wie steht es mit diesen Substantiven?

Gebrauche den *s*-Genitiv.

a man / world ______________________

women / magazines ______________________

a woman / job ______________________

men / hobbies ______________________

children / playground ______________________

a child / toys ______________________

people / ideas ______________________

girls / day ______________________

15 ★★☆ Vermischtes ...

Verbinde die Substantive mit dem *s*-Genitiv.

Are these your **teeth**? No, they are ______________________ (grandpa)

Is this your **baby**, Alice? No, it's my ______________________ (sister)

Are these your **parents**? No, they are ______________________ (Tom)

Are these your **jeans**? No, they are ______________________ (that girl)

Are these your **children**, Mrs Benson? No, they are ______________________ (Mr Owen)

Is that your **mum**, Ken? No, it's ______________________ (that boy)

Is this your hamster's **cage**? No, it's ______________________ (my parrot)

Is this your sister's **doll**? No, it's the ______________________ (twins)

Is this your child's **food**? No, it's ______________________ (the cat)

14 a man's world, women's magazines, a woman's job, men's hobbies, children's playground, a child's toys, people's ideas, girls' day

15 They are grandpa's teeth, … my sister's baby, …Tom's parents, … that girl's jeans, … Mr Owen's children, … that boy's mum, … my parrot's cage, … twins' doll, … the cat's food

16 ★★☆ Das Fragewort *whose*

Bilde den Genitiv der folgenden Substantive.
Beantworte die Fragen.

Whose car is this?	(Mr Benson)	______
Whose house is this?	(my parents)	______
Whose books are these?	(the girls)	______
Whose bike is this?	(Mike)	______
Whose pencils are these?	(Sue)	______
Whose wife is this?	(Mr Mason)	______
Whose girlfriend is this?	(Tom)	______
Whose trousers are these?	(my uncle)	______
Whose hat is this?	(grandma)	______

17 ★★☆ Wem gehört was?

Bilde Fragen mit *whose*.

______? This is Tom's girlfriend.

______? These are my toys.

______? That is your pen.

______? Those are the children's bikes.

______? This is her family.

______? This is my teacher's car.

______? These are my friends' friends.

______? This is Debbie's plate.

16 It's Mr Benson's car. It's my parents' house. These are the girls' books. This is Mike's bike. They are Sue's pencils. This is Mr Mason's wife. This is Tom's girlfriend. These are my uncle's trousers. This is my grandma's hat.
17 Whose girlfriend is this? Whose toys are these? Whose pen is that? Whose bikes are those? Whose family is this? Whose car is this? Whose friends are these? Whose plate is this?

18 ★★☆ Der *of*-Genitiv

Verbinde die folgenden Substantive mit dem *of*-Genitiv. Achte darauf, welches Substantiv zuerst kommen muss.

the table / the legs ______________________

the book / the month ______________________

your eyes / the colour ______________________

this book / the pages ______________________

the apple / my eye ______________________

the photos / my sister ______________________

the room / the walls ______________________

this house / the roof ______________________

the girl / my dreams ______________________

this word / the plural ______________________

this exercise / the end ______________________

19 ★★☆ Toms Freund

a) Unterstreiche das Genitiv-*s* mit einer anderen Farbe als das Apostroph-*s* der Kurzformen.

Tom's got a new friend. He's the new boy in Tom's class. Ken's family is new here, too. Ken's very good at maths. He can be very helpful, so most pupils in Tom's class like him. Ken's got a pet, too. It's a hamster. He must look after it, clean its cage and buy the hamster's food.

b) Schreibe die Kurzformen aus.

____

____

18 the legs of the table, the book of the month, the colour of your eyes, the pages of this book, the apple of my eye, the photos of my sister, the walls of the room, the roof of this house, the girl of my dreams, the plural of this word, the end of this exercise.

19 a) Tom**'s** got a new friend. He**'s** the new boy in Tom'<u>s</u> class. Ken'<u>s</u> family is new here, too. Ken**'s** very good at maths. He can be very helpful, so most pupils in Tom'<u>s</u> class like him. Ken**'s** got a pet, too. It**'s** a hamster. He must look after it, clean its cage and buy the hamster'<u>s</u> food.
b) Tom has got … He is the new boy … Ken is very good … Ken has got … It is a hamster.

20 ★☆☆ Der unbestimmte Artikel

Setze *a / an* vor die folgenden Substantive.

_______ name	_______ friend	_______ aunt
_______ year	_______ invitation	_______ game
_______ school	_______ example	_______ uncle
_______ teacher	_______ song	_______ exercise
_______ pupil	_______ unit	_______ pencil
_______ number	_______ question	_______ ruler
_______ uniform	_______ answer	_______ evening
_______ eye	_______ island	_______ library

21 ★☆☆ Was eine Übung alles sein kann ...

Setze den unbestimmten Artikel ein. Entscheide dich zwischen *a* oder *an*.

_______ useful exercise	_______ funny exercise	_______ beautiful exercise
_______ interesting exercise	_______ long exercise	_______ intelligent exercise
_______ complicated exercise	_______ short exercise	_______ important exercise
_______ difficult exercise	_______ good exercise	_______ bad exercise
_______ easy exercise	_______ German exercise	_______ awful exercise
_______ English exercise	_______ terrible exercise	_______ terrible exercise
_______ boring exercise	_______ silly exercise	_______ old exercise

20 a name, a year, a school, a teacher, a pupil, a number, a uniform, an eye; a friend, an invitation, an example, a song, a unit, a question, an answer, an island; an aunt, a game, an uncle, an exercise, a pencil, a ruler, an evening, a library

21 a useful exercise, an interesting exercise, a complicated exercise, a difficult exercise, an easy exercise, an English exercise, a boring exercise; a funny exercise, a long exercise, a short exercise, a good exercise, a German exercise, a terrible exercise, a silly exercise; a beautiful exercise, an intelligent exercise, an important exercise, a bad exercise, an awful exercise, an exciting exercise, an old exercise

22 ★★☆ Was ist das Gegenteil?

Finde das Gegenteil der hervorgehobenen Adjektive und setze die richtige Form des unbestimmten Artikels ein.

a **stupid** girl — an *intelligent* girl

a **difficult** question — ______________________

a **boring** lesson — ______________________

a **nice** boy — ______________________

a **happy** teacher — ______________________

a **cheap** pullover — ______________________

an **ugly** voice — ______________________

an **old** book — ______________________

a **terrible** boy — ______________________

23 ★★☆ Was weißt du noch?

Setze die Formen des unbestimmten Artikels ein und erkläre, wann du *a* oder *an* einsetzen musst.

Das nächste Wort beginnt mit:

______ girl — ______________________

______ bad girl — ______________________

______ interesting girl — ______________________

______ English girl — ______________________

______ uniform — ______________________

______ uncle — ______________________

22 an intelligent girl, an easy question, an interesting lesson, a terrible / silly / boy, an unhappy / a sad teacher, an expensive pullover, a beautiful voice, a new book, a nice boy

23 a, a, an, an, a, an. Das nächste Wort beginnt mit einem Konsonant, Konsonant, Vokal, Vokal, einem so genannten Halbvokal /ju/, Vokal.

24 ★★☆ Die Aussprache von *the*

a) Sprich die folgenden Beispielsätze laut aus.
Wann musst du den bestimmten Artikel / ðə /, wann / ði / aussprechen?

the English lesson

the boring biology lesson

the teachers at my school

the difficult questions

the interesting subjects

the easy tests

the exciting exercises

the unhappy pupils

the uniforms of English pupils

the old churches

b) Worauf kommt es bei dem bestimmten Artikel an? Gibt es Unterschiede zu den Regeln für den Gebrauch von *a / an*?

____

____

25 ★★☆ Ken ist krank

Ergänze jeweils den richtigen Artikel.

Today Ken is ill.

He has got ________ temperature.

He has got ________ sore throat.

He has got ________ headache, too.

Has he got ________ cold?

Well, I think he has got ________ bad cold, or he has got ________ flu.

It's ________ pity he can't come to our party.

24 a) Mit / ði / werden ausgesprochen: the English lesson, the easy tests, the exciting exercises, the unhappy pupils, the interesting subjects, the old churches.
Vor Vokal wird *the* wie / ði /, vor Konsonant und Halbvokal wie / ðə / ausgesprochen.
b) Es gelten dieselben Regeln wie für den Gebrauch von a / an.
25 He has got a temperature. He has got a sore throat. He has got a headache, too. Has he got a cold? Well, I think he has got a bad cold or he has got the flu. It's a pity he can't come to our party.

26 ★☆☆ Die Demonstrativbegleiter *this* und *that*

Setze in den Plural.

this family ______________________

that boy ______________________

this man ______________________

that lady ______________________

this class ______________________

that page ______________________

this foot ______________________

this child ______________________

this policewoman ______________________

that adult ______________________

this house ______________________

27 ★★☆ Erklärungen …

Setze die entsprechenden Formen von *this* ein.

__________ is a man and __________ are women.

__________ is a child and __________ are children, too.

__________ is a teacher and __________ are teachers, too.

__________ is a mouse and __________ are mice, too.

__________ is my friend and __________ are your friends.

26 these families, those boys, these men, those ladies, these classes, those pages, these feet, these children, these policewomen, those adults, these houses
27 This is a man and these are women. This is a child and these are children, too. This is a teacher and these are teachers, too. This is a mouse and these are mice, too. This is my friend and these are your friends.

28 ★★☆ Mein und dein

Setze die entsprechenden Formen von *this* und *that* ein.

__________ is my schoolbag and __________ is your schoolbag.

__________ is my seat and __________ is your seat.

__________ is my sandwich and __________ is your sandwich.

__________ are my books and __________ are your books.

__________ are my pencils and __________ are your pencils.

__________ are my CDs and __________ are your CDs.

__________ is my iPod and __________ is your iPod.

__________ are my things and __________ are your things.

__________ is my mobile and __________ is her mobile.

And __________ is my girlfriend; *don't think she is yours!*

29 ★★☆ Beim Einkaufsbummel

Ergänze die entsprechenden Formen von *this* und *that*.

Look at __________ pullover. It's really nice and __________ pullover is very nice, too.

Which pullover is nicer, __________ pullover or __________ pullover over there?

Look! Aren't they lovely? __________ t-shirts right in front of you?

And what about __________ t-shirts right here?

I like __________ t-shirts here better. Can we go in and buy one?

Okay, but let's have a look at __________ shirts in the shop window, too.

28 This is my schoolbag and that is your schoolbag. This is my seat and that is your seat. This is my sandwich and that is your sandwich. These are my books and those are your books. These are my pencils and those are your pencils. These are my CDs and those are your CDs. This is my iPod and that is your iPod. These are my things and those are your things. This is my mobile and that is her mobile. And this is my girlfriend; don't think she is yours!

29 Look at this pullover. It's really nice and that pullover is very nice, too. Which pullover is nicer, this pullover or that pullover over there? Look! Aren't they lovely? Those t-shirts right in front of you? And what about these t-shirts right here? I like these t-shirts here better. Can we go in and buy one? Okay, but let's have a look at those shirts in the shop window, too.

30 ★☆☆ Die Formen der Possessivbegleiter

Setze die passenden Possessivbegleiter ein.

This is *my* friend.	These are ________________ friends. (1. Person Plural)
This is *your* bike.	These are ________________ bikes. (2. Person Plural)
This is *his* car.	These are ________________ cars. (3. Person Plural)
This is *her* room.	These are ________________ rooms. (3. Person Plural)
This is *its* bone.	These are ________________ bones. (3. Person Plural)

31 ★☆☆ Der Possessivbegleiter *your*

Was kann *your* alles bedeuten? Übersetze.

What's *your* telephone number, Mrs Benson? ________________

When is *your* birthday, Tom? ________________

Where is *your* homework, Tom and Ken? ________________

Where's *your* car, Mr and Mrs Benson? ________________

Where's *your* workbook, Alice? ________________

32 ★★☆ Verwechsle *you* nicht mit *your*!

Setze die richtigen Formen ein.

How old are ______________, Alice?

Where are ________________ from?

Where is ______________ friend from?

Is she also in ________________ class?

Are Tom and Ken ________________ friends, too?

30 our friends, your bikes, their cars, their rooms, their bones
31 Ihre, dein, eure, Ihr, dein
32 How old are you? Where are you from? Where is your friend from? Is she also in your class? Are Tom and Ken your friends, too?

33 ★★☆ Wer hat was?

Setze die richtigen Formen des Possessivbegleiters ein.

1. I've got a bike. This is ____________ bike.
2. Sue has got a bike, too. That's ______________ bike.
3. Have you got a bike, Mrs Benson? Is that ____________ bike over there?
4. The saddle of the bike is new. ______________ saddle is new.
5. The Bensons have got a car. That's _______________ car.
6. We have got a new English book. This is _____________ new book.

34 ★★☆ Weitere Verwechslungsmöglichkeiten ...

Da hat doch jemand *its* mit *it's* verwechselt ... Korrigiere den Text. Ersetze *its* durch *it's*, wo *its* falsch ist.

Ken goes to a comprehensive school. **Its** a big school. **Its** a new school, too, but not everything is new. **Its** desks are old and a lot of **its** chairs are old, too. But many of **its** teachers are young. Ken likes it there. He thinks **its** a good school and that **its** fun to go there.

35 ★★☆ Und noch eine weitere Verwechslungsmöglichkeit

Wann ist *their* und wann ist *there* richtig? Setze die entsprechenden Formen ein.

Look, that's Tom's house over ____________.

Where? _______________, on your left.

That's _____________ house? Well, it's a big house.

Yes, and _______________ is a big garden behind it.

We often play _______________.

Oh, can we go _____________, too?

33 1. This is **my** bike. **2.** That's **her** bike. **3.** Is that **your** bike over there? **4. Its** saddle is new. 5. That's **their** car. **6.** This is **our** new book.
34 ... It's a big school. It's a new school, too ... He thinks it's a good school and that it's fun to go there.
35 Look, that Tom's house over there. Where? There, on your left. That's their house? ...There is a big garden behind it. We often play there. Oh, can we go there, too?

36 ★★★ Was weißt du noch?

Lies dir die folgenden Sätze genau durch und beantworte dann die folgenden Fragen:

Debbie is a **nice girl.** **She** is **nice.**

There are many **clever boys** in my class. **They** aren't all **stupid.**

	Richtig	Falsch
1. Adjektive beziehen sich immer nur auf Substantive.	●	●
2. Substantive können Sachen oder Personen sein.	●	●
3. Bei *to be* und einigen anderen Verben können Adjektive sich auch auf Pronomen beziehen.	●	●
4. Adjektive sind im Englischen unveränderlich.	●	●
5. Adjektive geben Eigenschaften der Personen oder der Sachen an, auf die sie sich beziehen.	●	●

37 ★★☆ Wie sie sein sollen oder wie sie sind ...

Wähle unter den folgenden Adjektiven drei aus, die die folgenden Personen charakterisieren.

nice, beautiful, good-looking, clever, crazy, exciting, fat, poor, rich, tall, short, strong, funny, interesting, boring, loud, difficult, old, young , sad, happy, loud, calm, stupid, intelligent, wonderful, uninteresting, aggressive, greedy, nervous, thin, funny

Beispiel: My favourite teacher: *He / she is old and loud, but very funny.*

My English teacher ______________________________

My maths teacher ______________________________

My mother ______________________________

My friend ______________________________

My __________ ______________________________

36 1. falsch (sie beziehen sich auch auf Pronomen, wie *she*), **2.** richtig, **3.** richtig, **4.** richtig, **5.** richtig
37 Mögliche Antworten: He / she is nice and young, but not very funny. He / she is young and clever, but not very exciting. She is good-looking and funny, but sometimes a bit loud. He is loud and strong, but very intelligent etc.

38 ★★☆ Welche Adjektive passen?

Welche Adjektive verbindest du mit den folgenden Substantiven? Notiere jeweils zwei.

Football? ______________________

Computers? ______________________

Boys? ______________________

Shopping? ______________________

Comics? ______________________

Pop stars? ______________________

Girls? ______________________

Casting shows? ______________________

English lessons? ______________________

39 ★★☆ Was ist das Gegenteil?

Setze bitte das entsprechende Adjektiv ein, um das Gegenteil zu bilden.

a new town ___an *old* town___

a thin boy ______________

a stupid girl ______________

a nervous boy ______________

a fast learner ______________

a poor man ______________

an easy exercise ______________

a tall man ______________

a large house ______________

an empty stomach ______________

a cheap ticket ______________

a long lesson ______________

an old woman ______________

a good girl ______________

38 Mögliche Antworten: Football is wonderful and exciting. Computers are useful and fast. Boys are loud and stupid. Shopping is boring and expensive. Comics are cheap and funny. Pop stars are crazy and often very loud. Girls are nice and good-looking. Casting shows are stupid and boring. English lessons are great, fantastic, exciting, wonderful!

39 an old town, a fat boy, an intelligent girl, a calm boy, a slow learner, a rich man, a difficult exercise; a short man, a small house, a full stomach, an expensive ticket, a short lesson, a young woman, a bad girl

40 ★★☆ Die Steigerung des Adjektivs

Bilde den Komparativ und den Superlativ der folgenden Adjektive.

rich ____________________ ____________________

cheap ____________________ ____________________

long ____________________ ____________________

loud ____________________ ____________________

41 ★★☆ Achte auf die Schreibung

Bilde, wie in Kurztest 40, den Komparativ und den Superlativ.

nice ____________________ ____________________

large ____________________ ____________________

big ____________________ ____________________

thin ____________________ ____________________

hot ____________________ ____________________

fat ____________________ ____________________

42 ★★☆ Und wie sieht es mit diesen Adjektiven aus?

Wie lauten der Komparativ und der Superlativ hier?

funny ____________________ ____________________

noisy ____________________ ____________________

busy ____________________ ____________________

easy ____________________ ____________________

lucky ____________________ ____________________

40 rich, richer, the richest; cheap, cheaper, the cheapest; long, longer, the longest; loud, louder, the loudest
41 nice, nicer, the nicest; large, larger, the largest; big, bigger, the biggest; thin, thinner, the thinnest; hot, hotter, the hottest; fat, fatter, the fattest
42 funny, funnier, the funniest; noisy, noisier, the noisiest; busy, busier, the busiest; easy, easier, the easiest; lucky, luckier, the luckiest

43 ★★☆ Adjektive mit drei oder mehr Silben

Wie lauten der Komparativ und der Superlativ hier?

famous ____________ ____________

boring ____________ ____________

expensive ____________ ____________

beautiful ____________ ____________

terrible ____________ ____________

44 ★★☆ Und nun wird es unregelmäßig …

Bilde die Steigerungsformen der folgenden Adjektive.

good ____________ ____________

bad ____________ ____________

much / many ____________ ____________

45 ★★☆ Was ist richtig?

Setze *most* oder *the most* ein.

____________ pupils think that homework is useless.

This is a mistake ____________ pupils make.

____________ mistakes are silly, but this mistake is ____________ idiotic.

Sheila is ____________ beautiful girl in our class. ____________ pupils like her.

Ben thinks that ____________ girls are stupid.

He only forgets that he is ____________ stupid boy in our class.

43 famous, more famous, the most famous; boring, more boring, the most boring; expensive, more expensive, the most expensive; beautiful, more beautiful, the most beautiful; terrible, more terrible, the most terrible
44 good, better, the best; bad, worse, the worst; much / many, more, the most
45 Most pupils think … This is a mistake most pupils make. Most mistakes … the most idiotic. Sheila is the most beautiful girl … Most pupils … Ben thinks that most girls … He only forgets that he is the most stupid boy in our class.

46 ★★☆ Alles zusammengefasst

Ergänze die Lücken entsprechend.

1. Adjektive mit einer Silbe und Adjektive mit zwei Silben, die auf *-y* und *-le* enden, bilden den Komparativ und den Superlativ mit *-er*, *-est*:

   cold ____________ ____________

   funny ____________ ____________

   simple ____________ ____________

2. Ein stummes *-e* am Ende des Adjektivs entfällt; nach Konsonant wird das *y* zu *i*:

   nice ____________ ____________

   easy ____________ ____________

3. Mit ganz wenigen Ausnahmen bilden alle anderen Adjektiven den Komparativ und den Superlativ mit *more*, *the most*:

   expensive ____________ ____________

   beautiful ____________ ____________

4. Einige ganz wenige Adjektive haben unregelmäßige Formen:

   good ____________ ____________

   bad ____________ ____________

47 ★★☆ Vermischtes . . .

Finde die Steigerungsformen der Adjektive.

dangerous ____________ ____________

dirty ____________ ____________

interesting ____________ ____________

careful ____________ ____________

quick ____________ ____________

46. 1. cold, colder, the coldest; funny, funnier, the funniest; simple, simpler, the simplest **2.** nice, nicer, the nicest; easy, easier, the easiest **3.** expensive, more expensive, the most expensive; beautiful, more beautiful, the most beautiful **4.** good, better, the best; bad, worse, the worst
47 dangerous, more dangerous, the most dangerous; dirty, dirtier, the dirtiest; interesting, more interesting, the most interesting; careful, more careful, the most careful; quick, quicker, the quickest

48 ★★☆ Steigerungen sind möglich …

Bilde Sätze mit den folgenden Angaben:

1. Bob / terrible boy / Danny / terrible + / John terrible ++

   Bob is a terrible boy, but Danny is more terrible. John is the most terrible boy of all.

2. This mistake / bad / that mistake + / those mistakes ++

   ____

3. Sue / smart girl / Alice + / Debbie ++

   ____

4. This test / difficult / the English test + / the maths test ++

   ____

5. Bob / noisy / his neighbour + / John ++

   ____

49 ★★☆ Vergleiche im Satz

Wähle ein Adjektiv aus und vergleiche. Gebrauche dabei *as … as* oder *not as … as*.

boring *interesting* *difficult* *bad* *intelligent*

football – tennis ______________________________

swimming – running ______________________________

English – German ______________________________

morning lessons – afternoon lessons ______________________________

books – comics ______________________________

I – my neighbour ______________________________

dolls – toy cars ______________________________

48 2. This mistake is bad. That mistake is worse, but those mistakes are the worst. **3.** Sue is a smart girl, but Alice is smarter. Debbie is the smartest girl of the three. **4.** This test is difficult, but the English test is more difficult. The maths test is the most difficult. **5.** Bob is noisy, but his neighbour is noisier. John is the noisiest of all.
49 Mögliche Antworten: Football is (not) as interesting as tennis. Swimming is (not) as boring as running. English is (not) as difficult as German. Morning lessons are (not) as bad as afternoon lessons. Books are (not) as interesting as comics. I am (not) as intelligent as my neighbour. Dolls are (not) as interesting as toy cars.

50 ★★☆ Genauso, aber anders …

Mache den vorigen Kurztest noch einmal, gebrauche aber *than*.

51 ★★☆ Mädchen und Jungs

Ersetze *not as … as* durch *than*, pass dabei aber auf den Sinn des Satzes auf.

Girls aren't as strong as boys.

Girls aren't as noisy as boys.

Boys aren't as good at learning languages as girls.

Boys aren't as difficult as girls.

Girls aren't as tough as boys.

50 Mögliche Antworten: Football is more interesting than tennis. Swimming is more boring than running. German is more difficult than English. Afternoon lessons are worse than morning lessons. Books are more interesting than comics. I am more intelligent than my neighbour. Dolls are more interesting than toy cars.
51 Boys are stronger than girls. Boys are noisier than girls. Boys are worse at learning languages than girls. Girls are more difficult than boys. Boys are tougher than girls.

52 ★★☆ Was ist richtig?

Setze *as (as … as)* oder *than* ein.

Are girls ________ intelligent ________ boys? Many people think girls are ________ intelligent, but others think that boys are more intelligent ________ girls. Just ask the boys in your class. They will tell you that boys aren't any better ________ girls, but secretly they think that they are the best. They can run faster ________ girls, they are stronger ________ girls, they are louder ________ girls and they are better at maths. Girls, they will say, are perhaps better in English ________ boys, but they are much worse in sports. What's your opinion? Do you think that girls are ________ clever ______ boys? Are they better or worse ________ boys?

53 ★★★ *Than, then* oder *as … as?*

Fülle die Lücken aus. Tipp: Denke dabei daran, dass *then* „dann, damals" heißt. Im Gegensatz dazu entspricht *than* dem deutschen „als" oder „wie" und kann nur im Vergleich gebraucht werden.

I tried to phone you yesterday, but you didn't answer the phone. What were you doing ________? I was reading a book ________. Reading a book? Was it so interesting? More interesting ________ the other one? Yes, it was. What was it about? It was about human intelligence, about the differences between men and women. Are there any? Aren't women ________ intelligent ________ men? Yes, they are. But in some fields men are better ________ women, in some fields they are ________ good ________ women and in some fields they are worse ________ women. Fine, ________ you seem to know everything about this problem …

52 Are girls as intelligent as boys? Many people think girls are as intelligent, … that boys are more intelligent than girls. … that boys aren't any better than girls, … They can run faster than girls, they are stronger than girls, they are louder than girls … Girls, they will say, are perhaps better in English than boys,… Do you think that girls are as clever as boys? Are they better or worse than boys?
53 What were you doing then? I was reading a book then. More interesting than the other one? Aren't women as intelligent as men? … men are better than women… they are as good as women … worse than women. Fine, then you seem to know …

54 ★☆☆ Mengenangaben mit *much / many*

a) Setze *much* oder *many* vor die folgenden Substantive.

________ food	________ people	________ water
________ wood	________ stories	________ countries
________ families	________ children	________ women
________ sugar	________ information	________ lemonade
________ years	________ tea	________ milk
________ courage*	________ pictures	________ coffee

b) Erkläre, weshalb du bei einigen Substantiven *much*, bei anderen *many* eingesetzt hast.

____

____

* courage = Mut

55 ★☆☆ Wunschträume …

Übersetze diese Ausdrücke. Gebrauche *much / many*.

viele Freunde ______________________________

viel Zeit ______________________________

viel Geld ______________________________

viele Partys ______________________________

viel Musik ______________________________

viel Spaß ______________________________

54 a) much food, much wood, many families, much sugar, many years, much courage; many people, many stories, many children, much information, much tea, many pictures; much water, many countries, many women, much lemonade, much milk, much coffee
b) *Many* steht bei Substantiven im Plural (zählbare Substantive z. B. *children*); *much* bei Substantiven, die im Englischen keinen Plural haben oder haben können (unzählbare Substantive z. B. *information*).
55 many friends, much time, much money, many parties, much music, much fun

56 ★★☆ Ein Schulfest

Setze die entsprechenden Formen von *much / many / a lot of* ein.

Today there is a big party at Tom's school. ___________ people are there. There are ___________ pupils of Tom's class, too. There are ___________ stalls there, too, where the pupils present their work. There is the photo club, for example. You can see ___________ photos at their stall. Then there is the rock club; they play ___________ music and have ___________ fun. They also have a chess club, where you can meet ___________ chess players and play against them. Then there is the bike club. There are ___________ bikes at their stall. The pupils there show you how to repair your bike, so ___________ pupils visit their stall.

57 ★★☆ Fragen

a) Setze *much / many / a lot of / lots of* richtig ein.

How ___________ is this bike? It costs too ___________ money!

How ___________ bikes have you got here?

How ___________ bikes can you repair in a day?

How ___________ money does it cost to repair a bike?

Are there any girls in the club, too? How ___________ girls are in your club?

How ___________ time do spend there? I spend so ___________ time there!

How ___________ pupils are in the club?

b) Wann kannst du *much* und *many* nicht durch *a lot of* ersetzen?

____

56 … Many / a lot of people are there, including many / a lot of pupils in Tom's class. There are many / a lot of stalls there, too … You can see a many / lot of photos at their stall. … they play a lot of music and have a lot of fun. They also have a chess club, where you can meet many / a lot of chess players … There are many / a lot of bikes at their stall. … so many / a lot pupils visit their stall.

57 a) How much is this bike? It costs too much money! How many bikes have you got here? How many bikes can you repair …? How much money does it cost …? How many girls …? How much time …? I spend so much time there! How many pupils …? **b)** Nach dem Fragewort *how*, und nach den Adverbien *so* und *too*, ist nur *much* oder *many* möglich.

58 ★★☆ Mengenangaben mit *a little, little, a few, few*

Übersetze die hervorgehobenen Begleiter.

I've got very **little** time today. ______

But I can find **a little** time for you. ______

I've got **a few** things to tell you. ______

Very **few** people know about this! ______

59 ★★☆ Was weißt du noch ...?

Vervollständige folgende Sätze.

Vor welchen Substantiven musst du **a little / little** und vor welchen Substantiven musst du **a few / few** gebrauchen?

a little / little steht vor Substantiven, die ______

a few / few steht vor Substantiven, die ______

Und was bedeutet **little** vor einem Substantiv, das einen Plural haben kann wie zum

Beispiel *girl*: She's my little girl ______

Handelt es sich hier auch um eine Mengenangabe? ○ Ja ○ Nein

60 ★★☆ Was braucht man für einen Ausflug?

Übersetze diese Ausdrücke.

ein paar Freunde ______

einige Sachen ______

sehr wenig Worte ______

ein bisschen Zeit ______

sehr wenig Hausaufgaben ______

58 wenig, ein bisschen, ein paar / einige, wenig(e)
59 … im Englischen keinen Plural haben (unzählbar sind); einen Plural haben (zählbar sind); mein kleines Mädchen; bei *my little girl* handelt es sich natürlich nicht um eine Mengenangabe.
60 a few / some friends, a few / some things, very few words, a little time, very little homework

61 ★★☆ Ein schön gedeckter Tisch

Sam, 3 Jahre alt, hat den Tisch gedeckt. Übersetze die hervorgehobenen Mengenwörter und das folgende Substantiv.

There are **some glasses** and **some spoons**, but there are**n't any knives** and forks on the table. There also is**n't any tea**, and there is**n't any sugar**. I ca**n't** see **any plates** either. Is there **any milk** on the table? Are there **any cups**? There is **some milk** on the table, but there is **no tea** and there are **no saucers**.

62 ★★☆ Was weißt du noch?

Entscheide, ob die folgenden Aussagen richtig oder falsch sind.

a) Die Bedeutung von **some** hängt davon ab, ob es vor einem Substantiv im Singular oder im Plural steht.

- richtig
- falsch

b) Vor einem Substantiv im Singular bedeutet **some** *etwas*, vor einem Substantiv im Plural *ein paar* oder *einige*.

- richtig
- falsch

c) Für **some** in der Bedeutung *ein paar / einige* kann ich auch **few** gebrauchen.

- richtig
- falsch

d) **Some** steht in nicht verneinten Aussagesätzen.

- richtig
- falsch

e) **not . . . any** bedeutet immer *kein(e)*.

- richtig
- falsch

f) Für **not . . . any** kann ich auch **no** gebrauchen.

- richtig
- falsch

g) Ein Satz kann auch mit **not . . . any** beginnen.

- richtig
- falsch

61 einige / ein paar Gläser, ein paar / einige Löffel, keine Messer, kein Tee, kein Zucker, keine Teller, (etwas) Milch, (irgendwelche) Tassen, (etwas) Milch, kein Tee, keine Untertassen.
62 a) richtig, **b)** richtig, **c)** falsch (richtig ist *a few*), **d)** richtig, **e)** richtig, **f)** richtig, **g)** falsch (mit *not … any* darfst du nie einen Satz beginnen).

63 ★★☆ Sag es anders

Ersetze *no* durch *not … any*.

	no friends.	______________________
	no money.	______________________
Mike has got	no parents.	______________________
	no brothers and sisters.	______________________
	no family.	______________________
	no food at home.	______________________
	no fun.	______________________

64 ★★☆ Gehen wir ins Kino!?

Setze die passenden Mengenwörter ein.

Is there ____________ good film on tonight?

Yes, there is. There's a good film in the Rex.

Okay, let's go there. Oh, but there's a problem. I haven't got ________ money on me.

I hope you have got ____________.

Sorry, I haven't. I haven't got ____________ money on me either.

What can we do then? Have you got ___________ ideas?

Let me think. Oh yes, let's ring up Alice. Perhaps she has got __________ money and can lend us ____________. Perhaps she can even come with us.

But Alice has got ___________ time and _________ money. She must do some babysitting because her parents are out. Poor Tom and Ken! They're not having

______________ luck tonight!

63 Mike hasn't got any friends / any money / any parents / any brothers and sisters / any family / any food at home / any fun.
64 Is there any good film on tonight? … I haven't got any money on me. I hope you have got some … I haven't got any money on me either. … Have you got any ideas? … Perhaps she has got some money and can lend us some … But Alice has got no time and no money. … Poor Tom and Ken! They're not having any luck tonight!

65 ★★☆ Sam

Setze die folgenden Begleiter so ein, dass der Text einen Sinn ergibt. Bei manchen Sätzen hast du mehrere Möglichkeiten.

many *a few* *some* *any* *a little* *much*

Sam is still a small boy. He can speak, but ______________ of his sentences are not correct. He makes ______________ mistakes. You need ______________ time to understand him. His real problem, however, is food. He only likes __________ things. ______________ vegetables are a real horror to him and he doesn't eat __________ meat. He also doesn't drink ______________ milk. What he likes, are sweets, but too ______________ sweets aren't good for him.

66 ★★☆ Zusammenfassung und Übersicht

Fülle die Tabelle richtig aus.

deutsche Bedeutung	Substantiv im Singular	Substantiv im Plural
viel(e)		
wenig(e)		
ein paar / einige		
ein bisschen		
etwas		
kein(e)		

65 … but many / a lot of / some / a few of his sentences are not correct. He makes many / a lot of / some / a few mistakes. You need a little / a lot of / some time to understand him. … He only likes a few / some things. Some / Many vegetables are a real horror to him and he doesn't eat any / a lot of meat. He also doesn't drink any / much milk. What he likes, are sweets, but too many sweets aren't good for him.

66

deutsche Bedeutung	Substantiv im Singular	Substantiv im Plural
viel(e)	much / a lot of	many / a lot of
wenig(e)	little	few
ein paar / einige	–	a few / some
ein bisschen	little	–
etwas	some	–
kein(e)	no / not … any	no / not … any

67 ★★☆ Sams Geburtstag

Setze die entsprechenden Begleiter ein.

There are ______________ children in the room. (viele)

______________ adults are there, too. (ein paar)

How ______________ children are there? (viele)

There is ______________ room left. (kein)

There are ______________ chairs left. (keine)

Most children are sitting on chairs, only ____________ are standing. (einige wenige)

Why is there so ______________ noise? (viel)

______________ children are shouting. (einige)

Why are so ______________ children there? (viele)

I have _______ got ______________ idea. (keine)

But wait, isn't it Sam's birthday? Yes, it is.

68 ★★☆ Was passt zusammen?

Ergänze die entsprechenden Mengenangaben.

a lot of homework → ______________ time

no work → ______________ money

many friends → ______________ fun

no friends → ______________ fun

a lot of money → ______________ friends

a lot of work → ______________ time

many sick teachers → ______________ school

67 There are many children in …, Some / a few adults …, How many children …?, … no room left, … no chairs left, … only a few are standing, … so much noise?, Some / a few children …, Why are so many …, I haven't got any idea.

68 a lot of homework = no / little time, no work = no money, many friends = a lot of fun, no friends = no fun, a lot of money = many friends, a lot of work = no / little time, many sick teachers = no school

69 ★★☆ Mengenangaben mit dem *of*-Genitiv

Verbinde die folgenden Mengenangaben mit einem passenden Substantiv.

a cup	of	shoes
a glass	of	bread
a bowl	of	cake
a plate	of	names
a piece	of	soup
a bag	of	lemonade
a slice	of	peas
a bar	of	chocolate
a tin	of	crisps*
a box	of	coffee
a bottle	of	butter
a pound	of	milk
a pair	of	oranges
a list	of	sausages

* crisps = Kartoffelchips (AmE: chips)

70 ★★☆ Hier stimmt was nicht

Korrigiere, was falsch ist. Verwende dabei andere Mengenangaben.

a box of water	a pound of milk
a glass of apples	a slice of toast
a tin of crisps	a box of cornflakes
a piece of tea	a bottle of chocolate

69 Mögliche Lösungen: a cup of coffee, a glass of milk, a bowl of soup, a plate of sausages, a piece of cake, a bag of crisps, a slice of bread, a bar of chocolate, a tin of peas, a box of oranges, a bottle of lemonade, a pound of butter, a pair of shoes, a list of names

70 a glass / cup / bottle of water; a box / pound of apples; a bowl / a bag of crisps; a cup / pot of tea; a bottle / glass of milk; a bar / piece of chocolate

71 ★☆☆ Mengenangaben mit Zahlen

Stelle die Fragen und beantworte sie. Beginne mit *there is / there are* . . .
Schreibe insgesamt 7 Sätze.

Beispiel: There are thirty-two pupils in my classroom.

How many	boys	are there	in your school?	
	girls		in your class?	
	desks		in your classroom?	
	pupils			
	teachers			
	windows			
	posters			

72 ★☆☆ Auch Schüler sind vergesslich . . .

Am Endes des Schuljahres werden die Sachen ausgelegt, die die Schüler während des Jahres vergessen haben . . . Schreibe auf, was sie liegen gelassen haben.

There are	15 pairs of trainers	in the caretaker's room.	
There is	2 right shoes		
	7 left shoes		
	4 shirts		
	6 anoraks		
	1 schoolbag		
	8 socks		
	5 English textbooks		

71 How many boys / girls / desks etc. are there in your school / class / classroom? There are ___ boys / girls / desks etc. in my school / in my class / in my classroom.
72 There are 15 pairs of trainers, two right shoes, seven left shoes, four shirts, six anoraks, eight socks and five English textbooks in the caretaker's room. There is also one schoolbag.

73 ★★☆ Eine üble Geschichte

Übersetze.

a) **Nobody** likes him. ______

b) He likes **nobody**. ______

c) He doesn't like **anyone**. ______

d) He doesn't like **anything**. ______

e) He likes **nothing**. ______

f) He goes **nowhere**. ______

g) He doesn't go **anywhere**. ______

h) You won't see him **anywhere**. ______

i) He doesn't want to see **anything**. ______

74 ★★☆ Sag es anders

Ersetze *nobody*, *nothing*, *nowhere*, wo dies möglich ist.

a) He likes nothing. ______

b) He likes nobody. ______

c) He does nothing. ______

d) He goes nowhere. ______

e) He is making nothing out of his life. ______

f) Nobody can help him. ______

g) Nothing can make him feel better. ______

h) You can do nothing about him. ______

73 a) niemand, **b)** niemanden, **c)** niemanden, **d)** nichts, **e)** nichts, **f)** nirgends, **g)** nirgends, **h)** nirgends, **i)** nichts
74 a) He doesn't like anything. **b)** He doesn't like anybody. **c)** He doesn't do anything. **d)** He doesn't go anywhere. **e)** He isn't making anything out of his life. **f)** nicht möglich **g)** nicht möglich. (Als Subjekt kann *nobody*, *nothing* nicht ersetzt werden.) **h)** You can't do anything about him.

75 ★★☆ Fragen und Antworten

Setze die Zusammensetzungen von *any* ein.

Does ______________________ know him? No, nobody knows him.

Has ______________________ seen him? No, nobody has seen him.

Did he go ______________________ ? No, he went nowhere.

Can you see him ______________________ ? No, I can't see him anywhere.

Did he do ______________________ ? No, he didn't do anything.

Did he talk to ______________________ ? No, he didn't talk to anybody.

76 ★★☆ Hilfe ...

Setze *jemand*, *etwas* etc. ein.

______________________ must talk to him. (jemand)

We must do ______________ about him. (etwas)

But what can we do? Can we really do ______________ ? (etwas)

We must find some help ______________________ . (irgendwo)

We must find ______________ to help him. (jemanden)

If we don't, ______________ terrible will happen. (etwas)

77 ★★★ Was weißt du noch?

Ergänze.

Wann musst du *some*, wann *any* gebrauchen? ______________________

Wann musst du *not* ... *any* gebrauchen? ______________________

75 Does anybody/anyone know him? Has anybody/anyone seen him? Did he go anywhere? Can you see him anywhere? Did he do anything? No, he didn't do anything. Did he talk to anybody/anyone?

76 Somebody/Someone must talk to him. We must do something about him. But what can we do? Can we really do anything? We must find some help somewhere. We must find somebody to help him. If we don't, something terrible will happen.

77 *Some* in bejahten Sätzen, *any* in Fragen; *not* ... *any* in verneinten Sätzen.

78 ★★★ *Some* und *somebody* in Fragen

a) Lies diese Sätze genau durch. Welche Antwort wird wohl erwartet?

Would you like something to drink?

Do you need some help in the kitchen?

Can I have some more coffee, please?

____

b) Trage *some* und die entsprechenden Zusammensetzungen ein.

Can I have ____________ money, please? You know, it's time for my pocket money.

Didn't I give you ____________ money yesterday? I really think I did. I hope you have got ____________ left.

Let's clean the car. Can ____________ come and help me? I really need ____________ help. Well, here's your chance. I'll give you ____________ extra money if you help me.

79 ★★☆ Hunger

Setze *everybody*, *everything* und *everywhere* ein.

____________ liked the food. There were lots of things: sausages, chips, peas, beans, just ____________! John, who was also at the party, looked at the food and liked ____________ he saw. As he was very hungry, he ate ____________ he could lay his hands on. When the party was over, all the plates were empty. But there was a lot of food on the floor. There were chips ____________. John was on the floor, too. He was sick. ____________ laughed at him.

78 a) Hier wird eine positive Antwort erwartet. **b)** Can I have some money, please? … Didn't I give you some money yesterday? I really think I did. I hope you have got some left. Let's clean the car. Can somebody / some-one come and help me? I really need some help. Well, here's your chance. I'll give you some extra money if you help me.

79 Everybody / Everyone liked the food. There were lots of things: sausages, chips, peas, beans, just everything! John … liked everything he saw. As he was very hungry, he ate everything he could lay his hands on. When the party was over, all the plates were empty. But there was a lot of food on the floor. There were chips everywhere. John was on the floor, too. He was sick. Everybody laughed at him.

80 ★☆☆ Telefonnummern

Wie lautet deine Telefonnummer? Kannst du sie auf Englisch sagen? Kannst du auch die folgenden Telefonnummern lesen?
(Tipp: BrE: 0 = oh, 00 = double oh; AmE: 0 = zero / oh, 00 = zero, zero / oh, oh)

Here's a list of the telephone numbers of Tom's friends:

Mike	57 97 91	
Debbie	30 06 90	mobile 0170 354 507 45
Alice	98 76 30	mobile 0510 809 607 543
Ken	24 39 19	
Kevin	92 95 28	
Ben	19 85 43	
Sue	70 08 03	

81 ★☆☆ Rätselhafte Zahlen

Bringe die Buchstaben in die richtige Reihenfolge.

fniefet ______________________

nttwey ______________________

eeetinnn ______________________

veenle ______________________

yeight ______________________

ddernuh ______________________

sadnuoht ______________________

eierntth ______________________

thtyir ______________________

80 five seven nine seven nine one, three double oh six nine oh; mobile oh one seven oh three five four five oh seven four five; nine eight seven six three oh; mobile oh five one oh eight oh nine six oh seven five four three; two four three nine one nine; nine two nine five two eight; one nine eight five four three; seven double oh eight oh three.

81 fifteen, twenty, nineteen, eleven, eighty, hundred, thousand, thirteen, thirty

82 ★★☆ Zahlenreihen

Lies die folgenden Zahlen laut. Welche Zahlen passen nicht zu den anderen? Schreibe sie auf.

a)	7	14	21	29	35	______
b)	9	18	27	37	45	______
c)	99	90	81	75	63	______
d)	77	71	63	56	49	______
e)	63	60	58	54	51	______
f)	12	18	25	30	36	______

83 ★★☆ Hier wird es schwieriger …

Lies die folgenden Zahlen laut und schreibe sie aus.

3	13	33
______	______	______
4	14	44
______	______	______
5	15	55
______	______	______
8	18	88
______	______	______
9	19	99
______	______	______

82 a) 29 – twenty-nine; **b)** 37 – thirty-seven; **c)** 75 – seventy-five; **d)** 71 – seventy-one; **e)** 58 – fifty-eight; **f)** 25 – twenty-five

83 three, thirteen, thirty-three; four, fourteen, forty-four; five, fifteen, fifty-five; eight, eighteen, eighty-eight; nine, nineteen, ninety-nine

84 ★☆☆ Die Uhrzeit

What time is it? **Schreibe die folgenden Uhrzeitangaben aus.**

6.00 ______________________________ 9.35 ______________________________

6.30 ______________________________ 10.20 ______________________________

6.45 ______________________________ 10.30 ______________________________

7.15 ______________________________ 11.40 ______________________________

8.50 ______________________________ 11.55 ______________________________

85 ★★☆ Toms Stundenplan für Montag

Schreibe den Stundenplan aus.

8.50 – 9.40	9.45 – 10.35	10.35 – 10.50	10.55 – 11.45
English	PE	break	Maths
11.50 – 12.40	**12.40 – 13.40**	**13.45 – 14.30**	**14.35 – 15.25**
Geography	lunch	Music	Art

Tom's first lesson is from ______________________ to ______________________.

PE is from ______________________ to ______________________.

Break is from ______________________ to ______________________.

Maths is from ______________________ to ______________________.

Geography is from ______________________ to ______________________.

Lunch break is from ______________________ to ______________________.

Music is from ______________________ to ______________________.

84 It's six o'clock; half past six (AmE = six thirty); a quarter to seven (AmE = six forty-five); a quarter past seven (AmE = seven fifteen); ten to nine (AmE = eight fifty); twenty-five to ten, thirty-five past nine (AmE = nine thirty-five); twenty past ten (AmE = ten twenty); half past ten (AmE = ten thirty); twenty to twelve (AmE = eleven forty); five to twelve (AmE = eleven fifty-five).

85 Tom's first lesson is from ten to nine to twenty to ten. PE is from a quarter to ten to twenty-five to eleven. Break is from twenty-five to eleven to ten to eleven. Maths is from five to eleven to a quarter to twelve. Geography is from ten to twelve to twenty to one. Lunch is from twenty to one to twenty to two. Music is from a quarter to two to half past two.

86 ★★☆ Der Busfahrplan von Bristol nach Clevedon

Lies den folgenden Busfahrplan laut und schreibe ihn dann aus.

10.31	10.48	10.53	11.02	11.08	11.13	11.24
Bristol, Bus Station	Wraxall	Nailsea	Tickenham Primary School	Clevedon, Kenn Road	Millcross	Clevedon, Cambridge Road

Beispiel: The bus leaves Bristol Bus Station *at ten thirty-one.*

It leaves Wraxhall ______________________.

It leaves Nailsea ______________________.

It leaves Twickenham Primary School ______________________.

It leaves Clevedon, Kenn Road, ______________________.

It leaves Millcross ______________________.

It arrives in Clevedon, Cambridge Road, ______________________.

87 ★★☆ Und wie steht es mit den folgenden Uhrzeiten?

Schreibe die folgenden Uhrzeiten aus. Setze *minutes* ein, wo dies notwendig ist.

5.35 ______________________

6.41 ______________________

7.25 ______________________

8.45 ______________________

8.46 ______________________

9.59 ______________________

11.19 ______________________

86 It leaves Wraxhall at ten forty-eight. It leaves Nailsea at ten fifty-three. It leaves Tickenham Primary School at eleven oh two. It leaves Clevedon, Kenn Road at eleven oh eight. It leaves Millcross at eleven thirteen. It arrives in Clevedon, Cambridge Road at eleven twenty-four.

87 It's twenty-five to six (AmE = five thirty-five). It's nineteen minutes to seven (AmE = six forty-one). It's twenty-five minutes past seven (AmE = seven twenty-five). It's a quarter to nine (AmE = eight forty-five). It's fourteen minutes to nine (AmE = eight forty-six). It's one minute to ten (AmE = nine fifty-nine). It's nineteen minutes past eleven (AmE = eleven nineteen).

88 ★☆☆ Große Zahlen ...

Schreibe die folgenden Zahlen aus.

100 ______________________________

200 ______________________________

345 ______________________________

888 ______________________________

1,000 ______________________________

2,000 ______________________________

100,000 ______________________________

1,000,000 ______________________________

89 ★★☆ Jahreszahlen

Weißt du noch, wie man Jahreszahlen liest? Es ist ganz einfach:

1492 *fourteen (hundred and) ninety-two*

1900 *nineteen hundred*

1648 *sixteen (hundred and) forty-eight*

2001 *two thousand one*

Lies und schreibe die folgenden Daten aus:

1776 ______________________________

2008 ______________________________

1888 ______________________________

1066 ______________________________

1668 ______________________________

1096 ______________________________

2049 ______________________________

88 a / one hundred, two hundred, three hundred and forty-five, eight hundred and eighty-eight, a / one thousand, two thousand, one hundred thousand, one million

89 seventeen hundred and seventy-six, two thousand eight, eighteen hundred and eighty-eight, ten hundred and sixty-six, sixteen hundred and sixty-eight, ten hundred and ninety-six, two thousand forty-nine

90 ★☆☆ Ordnungszahlen

Lies die folgenden Ordnungszahlen laut und schreibe sie aus.

1st the ____________________

2nd the ____________________

3rd ____________________

4th ____________________

5th ____________________

8th ____________________

9th ____________________

11th ____________________

12th ____________________

14th ____________________

15th ____________________

19th ____________________

20th ____________________

31st ____________________

44th ____________________

67th ____________________

91 ★☆☆ Ein Quiz

Beantworte die Fragen.

Which is the second month of the year? ____________________

What about December? Which month is it? ____________________

When is Christmas in English-speaking countries? On the ____________ of December.

And which is the fifth month? ____________________

Which is the eighth month? ____________________

And what about Tuesday? Which day of the week is it? ____________________

Which is the fifth day of the week? ____________________

Which is the first day of the week? ____________________

Look at Tom's timetable. Which lesson is Art? ____________________

And which lesson is Maths? ____________________

90 the first, the second, the third, the fourth, the fifth, the eighth, the ninth, the eleventh; the twelfth, the fourteenth, the fifteenth, the nineteenth, the twentieth, the thirty-first, the forty-fourth, the sixty-seventh
91 February, the twelfth month, twenty-fifth, May, August, the second day, Friday, Monday, the sixth lesson, the third lesson

92 ★★☆ Was sind das für Wochentage und Monatsnamen?

Schreibe sie richtig.

senadydwe ____________________

yrefabur ____________________

robetoc ____________________

thydrusa ____________________

omnyda ____________________

yuanajr ____________________

tugsua ____________________

syatruda ____________________

amcrh ____________________

ysetuda ____________________

93 ★★☆ Geburtstags-Tage!

An welchem Wochentag ist Toms Geburtstag dieses Jahr?

It's on a F ____________________.

And when is his father's? It's on a W ____________________.

And when is his mother's? It's on a Tu ____________________.

And when is his cousin's? It's on a Sa ____________________.

And when is his friend's? It's on a Th ____________________.

And when is Debbie's birthday? It's on a Su ____________________.

And when is your birthday this year? It's on ____________________.

92 Wednesday, February, October, Thursday, Monday, January, August, Saturday, March, Tuesday
93 It's on a Friday. It's on a Wednesday. It's on a Tuesday. It's on a Saturday. It's on a Thursday. It's on a Sunday. It's on a ____________.

94 ★★☆ Geburtstage

Schreibe die Geburtstage wie in dem folgenden Beispiel aus:

Tom, 12: *Tom is twelve. It's his twelfth birthday.*

His father, 39 — His mother, 37 — His uncle, 44

His aunt, 51 — His grandma, 72 — His grandpa, 78

His father ______________________________

His mother ______________________________

His uncle ______________________________

His aunt ______________________________

His grandma ______________________________

His grandpa ______________________________

95 ★★☆ Ein Geburtstagskalender

Lies den Geburtstagskalender laut und schreibe ihn entsprechend aus.

Tom, 2nd April: *Tom's birthday is on the second of April.*

His father, 11th August — His grandpa, 21st March — His uncle, 13th January

His mother, 14th July — His grandma, 19th May

His father's birthday is ______________________________

His mother's birthday is ______________________________

His uncle's birthday is ______________________________

His grandpa's birthday is ______________________________

His grandma's birthday is ______________________________

94 His father is thirty-nine; it's his thirty-ninth birthday. His mother is thirty-seven; it's her thirty-seventh birthday. His uncle is forty-four; it's his forty-fourth birthday. His aunt is fifty-one; it's her fifty-first birthday. His grandma is seventy-two; it's her seventy-second birthday. His grandpa is seventy-eight; it's his seventy-eighth birthday.

95 His father's birthday is on the eleventh of August. His mother's birthday is on the fourteenth of July. His uncle's birthday is on the thirteenth of January. His grandpa's birthday is on the twenty-first of March. His grandma's birthday is on the nineteenth of May.

96 ★★☆ Daten

Lies und schreibe die folgenden Daten aus.

17/12/1956

____

28/06/1940

____

25/07/2008

____

19/04/1913

____

03/12/2001

____

97 ★★☆ Öffentliche Feiertage in Great Britain

Kannst du die Feiertage den Daten zuordnen? Schreibe auf, was du gefunden hast.

New Year's Day	Boxing Day	Christmas Day	May Day	Summer Bank Holiday
27/08	1/5	1/1	25/12	26/12

New Year's Day is ______________________________

Boxing Day is ______________________________

Christmas Day is ______________________________

May Day is ______________________________

Summer Bank Holiday is ______________________________

96 The seventeenth of December, nineteen fifty-six; the twenty-eighth of June, nineteen forty; the twenty-fifth of July, two thousand eight; the nineteenth of April, nineteen thirteen; the third of December, two thousand one.

97 New Year's Day is on the first of January; Boxing Day is on the twenty-sixth of December; Christmas Day is on the twenty-fifth of December; May Day is on the first of May; Summer Bank Holiday is on the twenty-seventh of August.

98 ★★☆ Zeitangaben mit Präpositionen

Zeit- und Ortsangaben enthalten oft Präpositionen. Eine kleine Liste solcher Zeitangaben findest du hier. Setze die richtige Präposition ein.

____________ the morning
____________ the evening
____________ the afternoon
____________ three o'clock
____________ night
____________ Christmas
____________ three o'clock (vor)
____________ three o'clock (bis)
____________ my birthday
____________ the morning of my birthday
____________ February, 3rd
____________ December
____________ June
____________ 2008
____________ three o'clock (nach)
____________ morning ____________ night

99 ★★☆ Mein Tag

Ergänze die richtigen Präpositionen.

I usually don't go to bed ____________ 11 o'clock (vor).

I often go to bed ____________ midnight (nach).

I usually wake up ____________ 7 o'clock ____________ morning.

I leave the house ____________ breakfast (nach).

I have lunch ____________ about 1 o'clock.

I come home ____________ the late afternoon.

____________ the evening I often watch TV or read a book.

Things are different ____________ Sundays, of course.

98 in the morning, in the evening, in the afternoon, at three o'clock, at night, at Christmas, before three o'clock, until three o' clock (kann *by three o'clock* heißen, wenn man „bis spätestens" meint); on my birthday, on the morning of my birthday, on February, 3rd, in December, in June, in 2008, after three o'clock, from morning to night

99 I usually don't go to bed before 11 o'clock. I often go to bed after midnight. I usually wake up at 7 o'clock in the morning. I leave the house after breakfast. I have lunch at about 1 o'clock. I come home in the late afternoon. In the evening I often watch TV or read a book. Things are different on Sundays, of course.

100 ★★☆ Es gibt Leute, die gerne arbeiten …

Setze die richtigen Präpositionen ein.

I've got a friend who likes work very much. He works __________ morning _______ night. He works ________ the morning, ________ the afternoon, _________ the evening, even ________ Saturdays and _______ Sundays. He seldom goes to bed _______________ midnight (vor). He gets up very early, ______ about 6.

__________________ a short breakfast (nach) he settles down to work. Nothing can stop him. Last year he even worked ______________ his birthday and even ______________ December 25th, Christmas Day. Let's wish him a Merry Christmas this year!

101 ★★☆ Präpositionen

Ergänze die richtigen Präpositionen.

Tom was born ________ 1997.

His birthday is ________ April.

It is _________ April 2nd. His friend's birthday is _________ the same day.

It's _____________ a Friday this year.

_________ Saturday they are going to have a big party.

It's always fun to have parties _________ the weekend!

It will begin ____________ 3 o'clock and end _______ 11.

They'll prepare for the party __________ morning __________ night (von / bis) on Friday.

100 … He works from morning to night. He works in the morning, in the afternoon, in the evening, even on Saturdays and on Sundays. He seldom goes to bed before midnight. He gets up very early, at about 6. After a short breakfast he settles down to work. Nothing can stop him. Last year he even worked on his birthday and even on December, 25th, Christmas Day. Let's wish him a Merry Christmas this year!

101 Tom was born in 1997. His birthday is in April. It's on April 2nd. His friend's birthday is on the same day. It's on a Friday this year. On Saturday they are going to have a big party. It's always fun to have parties at the weekend! (AmE = on the weekend). It will begin at 3 o'clock and end at 11. They'll prepare for the party from morning to night on Friday.

102 ★★☆ Präpositionen

Was ist das Gegenteil von ...

on the left ____________

in front of the house ________ the house

on the table ____________

into the room ________ the room

over the house ________ the house

near the station far ________ the station

103 ★★☆ Toms Zimmer

Setze die folgenden Präpositionen ein. Manche kannst du mehrmals verwenden.

at *on* *above* *in* *in front of* *under* *next to* *behind*

Let's have a look ______ Tom's room. ______ the left there is his bed with a lamp ______ it. ______ the right there is a wardrobe. ______ the middle of the room there is a table and some chairs. There is one window ______ his room. ______ the window (vor) there is a desk with his schoolbooks ______ it. There is a computer ______ his desk, too. There are posters ______ the wall. But Tom's room is a mess. His socks are ______ his bed (unter) and his pullover is ______ the floor, too. There is an empty bottle of Coke ______ one corner of the room and there are many CDs ______ his bed (auf). Look! And what's that ______ the computer (hinter)? There is an old sandwich ______ an empty bag of chips (neben)!

102 on the right, behind the house, under the table, out of the room, under the house, far from the station.

103 Let's have a look at Tom's room. On the left there is his bed with a lamp above it. On the right there is a wardrobe. In the middle of the room … There is one window in his room. In front of the window there is a desk with his schoolbooks on it. There is a computer on his desk, too. There are posters on the wall … His socks are under his bed and his pullover is on the floor, too. There is an empty bottle of Coke in one corner of the room and there are many CDs on his bed. Look! And what's that behind the computer? There is an old sandwich next to an empty bag of chips.

104 ★★☆ Dein Zimmer

Beantworte die Fragen. Verwende eine der angegebenen Präpositionen.

Where is your bed?	(rechts / links / in der Mitte)
Where are your clothes?	(auf / unter / in).
Where are your posters?	(an) the wall.
Where is your desk?	(in der Mitte, links von, rechts von, vor)
What is ______ your desk?	(auf)
What is ______ your bed?	(hinter)

105 ★★☆ Wo sind sie?

Setze die fehlenden Präpositionen ein.

Where are the children? They are not ________________. They	zu Hause
are not ________ their room.	in
___________ the house there is a field. Are they playing	in der Nähe
____________ the field? It's not very _________ ________ the	auf / weit weg von
house.	
Or are they ______________ the street? There is a garden	auf
_________ the house. Are they there? No, they aren't.	um … herum
Where are they then? Oh, here they are. They are _______ the	in
living-room. Yes, they are. They are in the living room __________	vor
the telly. What film are they watching? It's a western. Look, here it is.	
It's ________ page 12 of the TV guide.	auf

104 It's on the right / on the left / in the middle. They are on / under / in the wardrobe. They are on the wall. It's in the middle, on the left, on the right, in front of … What is on your desk? What's behind your bed?
105 They are not at home. They are not in their room. Near the house there is a field. Are they playing in the field? It's not very far from the house. Or are they in the street? There is a garden round (AmE = around) the house … They are in the living-room in front of the telly …Oh, look, here it is, on page 12 of the TV guide.

106 ★★☆ Präpositionen, Präpositionen …

Setze die folgenden Präpositionen ein.

near *on* *at* *to* *into* *in front of* *out of* *under* *in*

It's already 8 o'clock. Tom's still __________ his room. He's packing his things for school. His English textbook is still __________ his desk. Some other books are lying __________ the floor __________ his bed. His pencil-case is also __________ the desk, __________ his computer. He's putting everything __________ his schoolbag. The bus is already waiting __________ the bus stop. Tom runs __________ the bus stop, but doesn't make it. So he has to go __________ school by bike. When he gets there, he rushes __________ the classroom, but he's late. His teacher is already there. He's standing __________ board with the register __________ his hands. A bit late, aren't you, Tom? You couldn't get __________ bed this morning, could you?

107 ★★★ Was sie bedeuten …

Ordne die Erklärungen den richtigen Präpositionen zu.

1. **to**	a) ist das Gegenteil von *into*
2. **in**	b) gibt an, dass sich etwas oder jemand auf ein Ziel hinbewegt
3. **into**	c) ist das Gegenteil von *above* und von *over*
4. **out of**	d) bedeutet immer *von irgendwo her* oder *weg von*
5. **from**	e) gibt an, dass jemand oder etwas in einem Raum ist
6. **at**	f) gibt an, dass jemand oder etwas in einen Raum hineingeht
7. **on**	g) jemand oder etwas befindet sich auf einer Oberfläche
8. **under**	h) gibt an, wo jemand oder etwas ist

106 … Tom's still in his room … His English textbook is still on his desk. … books are lying on the floor near / under his bed. His pencil-case is also on the desk in front of / near his computer. …everything into / in his schoolbag. The bus is already waiting at the bus stop. Tom runs to the bus stop, but he doesn't make it. So he has to go to school by bike. … he rushes into the classroom … He's standing in front of / near / at the board with the register in his hands … You couldn't get out of bed this morning, could you?

107 **1** b), **2** e), **3** f), **4** a), **5** d), **6** h), **7** g), **8** c)

108 ★☆☆ Das Personalpronomen als Subjekt

Übersetze die hervorgehobenen Formen.

I am Tom. __________

You are my sister. __________

You are right, Mr Owen. __________

You are right, Mr and Mrs Owen. __________

He is here. __________

She is at home. __________

It is on my desk. __________

We are at school. __________

You are wrong, Tim and Danny. __________

You don't like her, do you, John? __________

They are here. __________

109 ★★☆ Was weißt du noch?

Beantworte die folgenden Fragen.

a) Wann gebrauchst du diese Pronomen? Als Objekt oder als Subjekt eines Satzes?

____

b) Was musst du dir bei **I** merken?

____

c) Wie viele unterschiedliche Bedeutungen hat **you**? Nenne sie!

____

d) Welche Substantive kannst du durch **it** ersetzen? Unterstreiche sie.

food, cats, house, sister, girl, ball, desks, school, teacher, pupil, pages, door

108 ich, du, Sie, Sie, er, sie, es, wir, ihr, du, sie
109 a) als Subjekt eines Satzes; **b) I** wird immer großgeschrieben. **c)** drei Formen (du, ihr, Sie); **d)** food, house, ball, school, door

110 ★★☆ *You, they oder she?*

Setze die richtigen Pronomen ein.

It's really nice to see ________, Mrs Owen.

How are ________, Mrs Owen?

Are ________ all right?

And how is Alice? Is ________ all right?

How old is ________ now?

Is ________ here, too?

Where are your bags? Are ________ still in the car?

111 ★★☆ Vor der Schule

Tom sucht nach seinen Sachen …
Ersetze das hervorgehobene Substantiv durch ein Pronomen.

Where is **my schoolbag**? ________ is here.

Where are **my pencils**? ________ are over there.

Where is **my paper**? ________ is here on the table.

Where are **my pen and my ruler**? ________ are over there.

Where are **my books**? ________ are on the shelf.

Where is **my English exercise-book**? ________ is in your schoolbag.

Where is **my biro***? ________ is on your desk.

Where is **my German textbook**? ________ is on your desk, too.

Where is **my money**? Is ________ on my desk, too?

Can ________ have it?

* AmE = ballpoint pen

110 It's nice to see you, Mrs Owen. How are you, Mrs Owen? Are you all right? … Is she all right? How old is she now? Is she here, too? … Are they still in the car?
111 It …, They …, It …, They …, They …, It …, It …, It …, Is it …?, Can I have it?

112 ★★☆ In der Schule

Setze das richtige Pronomen ein.

Hello, ______ am Tom.

Are ________ new here?

Where are __________ from?

What about your parents? Are _________ from Bristol, too?

Is that your bike? Is _________ new?

Have ______ got a sister?

How old is ______?

Is _________ in your class?

Is _________ nice?

Can __________ meet her?

113 ★★☆ Während einer Englischstunde …

Setze die richtigen Pronomen ein.

Where is your homework, Tom?

_______ is not here. _______ can't find it. ______ must still be on my desk.

And where is your homework, Danny? Is ________ at home, too?

No, Sir, _______ think ______ is on the bus.

What are ________ doing, Alice and Sue? Are ________ doing your homework now?

No, sir, _________ are just writing a letter.

What! ________ are writing a letter during the English lesson?

Yes, Sir, __________ are.

112 I am Tom. Are you new here? Where are you from? … Are they from Bristol, too? … Is it new? Have you got a sister? How old is she? Is she in your class? Is she nice? Can I meet her?
113 It is not here. I can't find it. It must still be on my desk. … Is it …? I think it is on the bus. What are you doing …? Are you doing …? No, sir, we are … What! You are … Yes, sir, we are.

114 ★☆☆ Die Formen des Personalpronomens als Objekt

Trage die entsprechenden Objektformen des Personalpronomens ein.

Singular:			Plural:	
I	______	→	we	______
you	______	→	you	______
he	______	→	my uncles/they	______
she	______	→	my aunts/they	______
it	______	→	my cats/they	______

115 ★★☆ Das Pronomen *you*

Welche Bedeutung hat *you* in diesen Sätzen?

a) **You** are right, Tom. ______

You are right, Tom and Jerry. ______

You are right, Mr Owen. ______

You are right, Mr and Mrs Owen. ______

b) I can't help **you**, Tom. ______

I can't see **you**, Tom. ______

I can't help **you**, Tom and Jerry. ______

I can't see **you**, Mr Owen. ______

I can't help **you**, Mr. Owen. ______

I can't see **you**, Mr and Mrs Owen. ______

I can't help **you**, Mr and Mrs Owen. ______

114 me, you, him, her, it; us, you, them, them, them
115 a) du, ihr, Sie, Sie; **b)** dir, dich, euch, Sie, Ihnen, Sie, Ihnen

116 ★★☆ Und wie steht es mit den anderen Objektformen?

Wie heißen sie auf Deutsch? Schaue dir die folgenden Sätze an.

He can see **me / him / her / it**.

He can help **me / him / her / it**.

He can see **us / them**.

He can help **us / them**.

me ______ / ______

him ______ / ______

her ______ / ______

it ______ / ______

us ______ / ______

them ______ / ______

117 ★★☆ Während der Pause …

Tom ist wieder auf der Suche. Beantworte Toms Fragen.

I can't see … *I can't find …*

Where is **my schoolbag**? ______

Where is **my chewing-gum**? ______

Where are **my sandwiches**? ______

Where is **my money**? ______

Where is **Alice**? ______

Where is **that new boy**? ______

Where are **the others**? ______

Where is **my anorak**? ______

Where are **my glasses**? ______

Where is **my scarf**? ______

And where are **my shoes**? ______

116 mich / mir; ihn / ihm; sie / ihr; es / ihm; uns / uns; sie / ihnen
117 I can't see / find it, it, them, it, her, him, them, it, them, it, they

118 ★★☆ Spaß in der Pause

Setze die richtigen Pronomen ein.

Let _______ play together. What game can _____ play? We can play football!

Oh, but then _____ need two more people.

Then let _____ look for Tom and Danny.

Where are __________? I can't see ___________.

Oh, look, __________ are over there.

Let _______ go and talk to ______________.

Hey, Tom and Dan, can you play with _____?

No, _____ can't. Can't __________ see that ________ are busy?

What are ___________ doing?

Well, can ___________ see those girls over there? _____ are watching _______.

119 ★★☆ Hausaufgaben

Setze die richtigen Pronomen ein.

I've got a problem, Dad. Can _____ help ______?

Sorry, son. _____ have got no time. Ask your mother. Perhaps _____ can help _______.

But Tom's mother is busy, too. So ____________ says to Tom: Oh, sorry, Tom. _____ really can't. __________ must go shopping. Ask your sister.

But Tom's sister is not at home. So __________ can't ask ___________.

Poor Tom! What can _____ do? Can ______ ask his teacher? His teacher will perhaps be angry with __________.

118 Let us / let's play together / What game can we play? … But then we need two more people. Then let us look for Tom and Danny. Where are they? I can't see them. Oh, look, they are over there. Let us / let's go and talk to them. Hey, Tom and Dan, can you play with us? No, we can't. Can't you see that we are busy? What are you doing? Well, can you see those girls over there? We are watching them.

119 Can you help me? Sorry, son. I have got no time … Perhaps she can help you. But Tom's mother is busy. So she says to Tom: … I really can't. I must go shopping. … So he can't ask her. … What can he do? Can he ask his teacher? His teacher will perhaps be angry with him.

120 ★★☆ Was weißt du noch?

Übersetze die folgenden Fragen und beantworte dann die Frage zur Grammatik.

a) Can you help **me**? ______________________

b) Can you see **me**? ______________________

c) Can you go **with me**? ______________________

Wann musst du den Objektfall des Personalpronomens gebrauchen?

a) für ein Substantiv im ______________________

b) für ein Substantiv im ______________________

c) für ein Substantiv nach einer ______________________

121 ★★☆ Versteckspiel

Setze die entsprechenden Pronomen ein.

Where are Alice and Ken? Everybody is looking for _______, but nobody can find _______. Where are _______ hiding? The children are looking for Alice first. Where is _______? Is _______ in Tom's room? No, _______ isn't in the room. _______ is empty. There is no trace of* _______ there. Is _______ under Tom's bed? No, _______ isn't. Is _______ behind the door? No, _______ isn't. _______ isn't behind _______. Where is _______ then? _______ is in the wardrobe, with Ken! _______ are hiding behind some clothes, so nobody can find _______. But _______ are laughing, so the children can hear _______.

* There is no trace of … = Da ist keine Spur von …

120 a) im Wem-Fall (= Dativ); **b)** im Wen-Fall (= Akkusativ); **c)** nach einer Präposition

121 … Everybody is looking for them, but nobody can find them. Where are they hiding? The children are looking for Alice first. Where is she? Is she in Tom's room? No, she isn't in the room. It is empty. There is no trace of her there. Is she under Tom's bed? No, she isn't. Is she behind the door? No, she isn't. She isn't behind it. Where is she then? She is in the wardrobe, with Ken! They are hiding behind some clothes, so nobody can find them. But they are laughing, so the children can hear them.

122 ★☆☆ Wie lauten die Formen?

Ersetze die Substantive mit dem Possessivbegleiter durch das entsprechende Pronomen.

This is **my pen.**	It's ______________________.
Is this **your pen**?	Is it ______________________?
That's **her bag.**	That's ______________________.
That's **his book.**	That's ______________________.
This is **our dog.**	It's ______________________.
Is this **your car**?	Is this ______________________?
Are these **their bikes**?	Are these ______________________?

123 ★★☆ In der Schulcafeteria

Setze die entsprechenden Possessivpronomen ein.

This is not your table. We are sitting here. This table is ________________.

You sit over there! ________________ is over there.

Hey, that's my chair, Ben. It isn't ________________.

Those aren't your seats, Ken und Sam. ________________ are over there.

Is this your glass? No, it isn't. It belongs to Alice. It's ________________.

And this plate? Is it yours, Debbie? Yes, it's ________________.

And what about this plate? Is it Tom's? Yes, it is. It's ________________.

Don't eat those chocolate puddings! Mike and Ken put them on the table.

They are ________________.

Is that your purse? I don't think it's ________________. It must be Debbie's.

Yes, it's ________________.

122 mine, yours, hers, his, ours, yours, theirs
123 … This table is ours. Yours is over there. … Ben. It isn't yours. Those aren't your seats, Ken und Sam. Yours are over there. Is this your glass? No, … It's hers. … Debbie? Yes, it's mine. … Yes, it is. It's his. …They are theirs. … I don't think it's mine. … Yes, it's hers.

124 ★★☆ Auf der Suche …

Ergänze die Possessivpronomen.

a) Look at these shoes! I don't think they are ____________; they aren't my size.

But, perhaps they are ____________, Tom. They really look as if they could be ____________.

No, they aren't. I never forget my trainers. I always keep ____________ in my locker.

b) Debbie, look here. Isn't Alice missing a blouse? Couldn't that be hers? I don't really think that blouse is ____________. It's too small.

c) Oh look, Betty. Aren't Sue and Mary looking for their English books? The books over there could be ____________. Let's see if we find their names in them. Oh no, they aren't ____________. They're ours!

d) And what about those socks over there? Oh, they smell rather bad. Then they are Bob's socks. We should tell him that the socks over here are ____________.

125 ★★★ Typische Fehler

Kennst du die richtige Form?

Er ist ein Freund **von mir***.	He's a friend ____________.
Sie ist eine Kollegin **von dir**, oder?	She's a colleague ____________, isn't she?
Ist Tom ein Freund **von ihm**?	Is Tom a friend ____________?
Nein, Tom ist ein Freund **von ihr**.	No, Tom's a friend ____________.
Sie sind Kollegen **von uns** …	They are colleagues ____________.
… und auch Kollegen **von euch**!	… and colleagues ____________, too!
Seid ihr auch Freunde **von ihnen**?	Are you also friends ____________?

Typischer Fehler: "a friend from me" würde heißen, dass er ein Freund ist, den ich jemandem geschenkt habe!

124 a) … they aren't mine. … perhaps they are yours, Tom. … as if they could be yours. … I always keep mine in my locker. **b)** … that blouse is hers. **c)** … could be theirs. … they aren't theirs. **d)** … the socks over there are his.
125 of mine, of yours, of his, of hers, of ours, of yours, of theirs.

126 ★★☆ Shopping

Ersetze die hervorgehobenen Substantive.

Look at these pullovers. Do you like them? Which **pullovers**? ____________________

The green **pullover** and the blue **pullover** over there. ____________________

No, I don't like them, but look at that red **pullover**. I like that one a lot! ______________

I know that red is your favourite colour.

But why don't you like that **pullover** over there? ____________________

You mean the yellow **pullover**? ____________________

Yes, that **pullover**. The **pullover** with Big Ben on it. ____________________

Okay, it's not too bad.

Okay, then let's go in and try on that yellow **pullover**. ____________________

127 ★★☆ Im Laden

Unterstreiche die Substantive, bei denen das Ersetzen sinnvoll ist.

Excuse me, could I try on that yellow pullover?

Which pullover?

The pullover over there with Ben Big on it.

Here you are. Try it on, if you like.

I like it, but it's a bit too small. Haven't you got a bigger pullover?

No, I'm afraid not*. That's the only pullover left.

Okay, could you show me the red pullover over there?

Sure I can. Just try it on.

Oh, I like this pullover very much. And how much is it? I'll take it. I love red pullovers.

* I'm afraid not = Leider nicht

126 Which ones? The green one and the blue one ... Look at the red one. ... that one over there? ... the yellow one. Yes, that one. The one with Beg Ben on it. ... that yellow one.

127 Excuse me, could I try on that yellow pullover? Which one? The one over there with Ben Big on it. ... a bigger one? ... the only one left. ... show me the red one over there? ... Oh, I like this one very much.

128 ★☆☆ Schüttelreime

Setze die fehlenden Formen von *to be* ein.

We ________ happy
We ________ proud.
Our teachers ________ too loud.

We ________ late
That ________ all right.
School can wait!

Girls ________ nice,
or cold as ice.
And Sally has got a dirty face!

You ________ right,
and I ________ wrong.
But my brother ________ very strong!

129 ★☆☆ Ein neuer Schüler

Schreibe die Kurzformen in Langformen um.

Hi, I'm Danny. ______________________________

I'm from Sheffield. ______________________________

My parents? They're from Sheffield, too. ______________________________

We're new here. ______________________________

And who's that in that photo? ______________________________

That's my sister. ______________________________

She's ten. ______________________________

128 We are happy
We are proud.
Our teachers are too loud.
We are late
That's all right.
School can wait

Girls are nice,
or cold as ice.
And Sally has got a dirty face!
You are right,
and I am wrong.
But my brother is very strong!

129 I am Danny. I am from Sheffield. They are from Sheffield, too. We are new here. And who is that in that photo? That is my sister. She is ten.

130 ★☆☆ In der Schule

Setze die richtigen Formen von *to be* ein.

________ you new here?

What _____ your name?

How old ___________ you?

Where ________ you from?

What about your parents? _________ they from Sheffield, too?

________ that your bike? _________ it new?

_________ that your sister? _________ she in your class?

What about her friends? They _________ very nice.

________ I right?

131 ★★☆ Ganz falsch ...

Setze die richtigen Formen von *to be* ein. Einige Formen werden verneint.

Sorry, I ____________ not Ken, I ________ Tom.

You're from Bristol, right? We _____________ from Bristol, we ________ from York.

_______ you new here? Yes, we ___________.

______ the girl over there your sister? No, she ________. She ___________ my sister.

________ she in your class? No, she _______________ in my class. She ________ in my sister's class.

What about the boys over there? _______ they in your class? They ___________ in my class either.

And the man over there? He ________ our teacher. He _________ our caretaker.

130 Are you new here? What is your name? How old are you? Where are you from? Are they from Sheffield, too? Is that your bike? Is it new? Is that your sister? Is she in your class? They are very nice. Am I right?
131 Sorry, I am not Ken, I am Tom. … We aren't from Bristol. We are from York. Are you new here? Yes, we are. Is the girl over there your sister? No, she isn't. She isn't my sister. Is Tanya in your class? No, she isn't in my class. She is in my sister's class. … Are they in your class? No, they aren't in my class either. … He is our teacher. He is our caretaker.

132 ★★☆ Dannys Fragen

Danny ist total durcheinander. Stelle seine Fragen.

you / Excuse me / Tom / are? ______________________________?

you / are / from Bristol? ______________________________?

that / your sister / is? ______________________________?

she / in your class / is? ______________________________?

what / her name / is? ______________________________?

how / is / she / old? ______________________________?

these boys / in your class / are / too? ______________________________?

your classroom / is / that? ______________________________?

the man over there / a teacher / is? ______________________________?

133 ★★☆ Fragen über Fragen

Gib Kurzantworten.

a) Are you often late? No, ____________________.

b) Are your teachers always late? No, ____________________.

c) Are your friends happy? Yes, ____________________.

d) Are you and your friends happy? Yes, ____________________.

e) Are you a nice and friendly person? Yes, ____________________.

f) Are you a good pupil? Yes, ____________________.

g) Are your marks always good? Yes, ____________________.

h) Is this exercise difficult? No, ____________________.

i) And your school reports? Are they good? Yes, of course ____________________!

132 Excuse me, are you Tom? Are you from Bristol? Is that your sister? Is she in your class? What is her name? How old is she? Are these boys in your class, too? Is that your classroom? Is the man over there a teacher?
133 a) No, I'm not. **b)** No, they aren't. **c)** Yes, they are. **d)** Yes, we are. **e)** Yes, I am. **f)** Yes, I am. **g)** No, they aren't. **h)** No, it isn't. **i)** Yes, of course they are!

134 ★☆☆ Ein Klassenzimmer

Entscheide, ob diese Sätze mit *there is* oder *there are* gebildet werden.

________________ lamps

________________ a lot of desks

________________ windows in the classroom.

________________ a lot of chairs

________________ a board

________________ a mirror

________________ posters

135 ★★☆ Dein Zimmer

Gib eine Kurzantwort, beantworte aber anschließend die Frage mit der Information in Klammern in einem ganzen Satz.

Beispiel: Is there a bed in your room? (ja, 2) *Yes, there is. There are two beds in my room.*

Is there a wardrobe in your room? (ja, 1) ________________

Are there books in your room? (nein) ________________

Is there a computer in your room? (ja, 1) ________________

Are there chairs in your room? (ja, 3) ________________

Is there a toilet in your room? (nein) ________________

Is there a lamp in your room? (ja, 2) ________________

Is there a TV set in your room? (ja, 1) ________________

134 There are lamps / There are a lot of desks / There are windows / There are a lot of chairs / There is a board / There is a mirror / There are posters in the classroom.

135 Yes, there is. There is one / a wardrobe in my room.; No, there aren't. There aren't any books in my room.; Yes, there is. There is one / a computer in my room.; Yes, there are. There are three chairs in my room.; No, there isn't. There isn't a toilet / There is no toilet in my room.; Yes, there is. There are two lamps in my room.; Yes, there is. There is one / a TV set in my room.

136 ★★☆ Deine Schule

Gib Kurzantworten auf Fragen mit *there is / there are*.

Are there many pupils at your school? ______________________

Are there many boys in your class? ______________________

Are there any nice girls / boys in your class? ______________________

Is there a cafeteria at your school? ______________________

Is there a gym, too? ______________________

Is there an outdoor swimming pool, too? ______________________

Are there many activities at your school? ______________________

Is there a theatre group or a photo club? ______________________

137 ★★☆ Fragen mit *that*

Gib Kurzantworten.

Is that an English book? Yes, ______________________.

Is that an interesting book? No, ______________________.

Is that your teacher? Yes, ______________________.

Is that Mr Mason? Yes, ______________________.

Is that your school? No, ______________________.

Is that your boyfriend? Yes, ______________________.

Is that your girlfriend? No, ______________________.

Is that a silly question? Yes, ______________________.

136 Mögliche Antworten: Yes, there are. / No, there aren't.; Yes, there are. / No, there aren't; Yes, there are. / No, there aren't.; Yes, there is. / No, there isn't.; Yes, there is. / No, there isn't.; Yes, there is. / No, there isn't.; Yes, there are. / No, there aren't.; Yes, there is. / No, there isn't.

137 Yes, it is.; No, it isn't.; Yes, it is.; Yes, it is.; No, it isn't.; Yes, it is.; No, it isn't.; Yes, it is.

138 ★★☆ Während der Mittagspause

Gib Kurzantworten.

Isn't that Mr Mason? Yes, ______________________.

Isn't he your English teacher? Yes, ______________________.

Aren't you happy to see him? No, ______________________.

Is that your school cafeteria? Yes, ______________________.

What about the food there? Is it good? No, ______________________.

Are there any good restaurants here? No, ______________________.

Is that a good restaurant? No, ______________________.

Are you hungry? Yes, ______________________.

139 ★★☆ Sei neugierig!

Stelle Fragen und gib Kurzantworten.

Frag deinen Freund,

1. ob er ein guter Schüler ist: *Are you a good pupil? Yes, I am. / No, I'm not.*
2. ob er glücklich ist: ______________________
3. ob seine Lehrer nett sind: ______________________
4. ob seine Schule groß ist: ______________________
5. ob sein Englischlehrer gut ist: ______________________
6. ob sein Unterricht (= lessons) langweilig ist: ______________________
7. ob viele Jungen in seiner Klasse sind: ______________________

138 Yes, it is.; Yes, he is.; No, I'm not.; Yes, it is.; No, it isn't.; No, there aren't.; No, it isn't.; Yes, I am.
139 2. Are you happy? Yes, I am. / No, I'm not. **3.** Are your teachers nice? Yes, they are. / No, they aren't. **4.** Is your school large/big? Yes, it is. / No, it isn't. **5.** Is your English teacher good? Yes, he is. / No, he isn't. **6.** Are his lessons boring? Yes, they are. / No, they aren't. **7.** Are there many boys in your class? Yes, there are. / No, there aren't.

140 ★★☆ Fragen mit Fragewörtern

Stelle Fragen mit den Fragewörter *who, how, what, where*.

___________ are you?	I'm Tom.
___________ are you?	Fine, thanks. And you?
___________ is his name?	His name is Ken.
___________ is your friend?	Danny is my friend.
___________ old are you?	I'm twelve.
___________ are the other boys?	They are at school.
___________ is your bike?	It's right there.
___________ is your sister?	She's at home.
___________ is your English teacher?	Mr Mason is my English teacher.
___________ is that on your chair?	It's a book.
___________ kind of book is it?	It's an English book.

141 ★★☆ Und nun auf Deutsch!

Übersetze die folgenden Sätze!

Wo bist du? ___________________________

Wie heißt du? ___________________________

Wo bist du her? ___________________________

Wie heißt dein Vater? ___________________________

Wie alt bist du? ___________________________

Wo sind deine Eltern? ___________________________

Wer ist dein Freund? ___________________________

140 Who are you? How are you? What is his name? Who is your friend? How old are you? Where are the other boys? Where is your bike? Where is your sister? Who is your English teacher? What is that on your chair? What kind of book is it?
141 Where are you? What's your name? Where are you from? What's your father's name? How old are you? Where are your parents? Who is your friend?

142 ★☆☆ Was sie alles haben

Setze die richtigen Langformen von *have got* ein.

Mr and Mrs Benson ____________ a son.

They ____________ a daughter, too.

Mr Benson ____________ an interesting job.

The Bensons ____________ a house.

They ____________ a car, too.

Mrs Benson ____________ got a sister.

She ____________ a nice house in the country.

She ____________ two children, too.

143 ★☆☆ Und wie steht es mit dir?

Schreibe über deine Familie. Gebrauche die Kurzformen.

I ______________________________.

My mother / father ______________________________.

She / he ______________________________, too.

My sister / brother ______________________________.

He / she ______________________________, too.

We ______________________________.

My uncle and my aunt ______________________________.

My cousin / cousins ______________________________.

142 Mr and Mrs Benson have got a son. They have got a daughter, too.; Mr Benson has got an interesting job. The Bensons have got a house. They have got a car, too. Mrs Benson has got a sister. She has got a nice house in the country. She has got two children, too.

143 I've got …; My mother's got … / My father's got …; She's got … / He's got …; My sister's got … / My brother's got …; He's got … / She's got …; We've got …; My uncle and my aunt have got …; My cousin has got … / My cousins have got …

144 ★★☆ Nicht jeder hat alles ...

Schreibe auf, was sie haben und was nicht.

Sam	Ken	The Bensons	Emma	Alice
~~brother~~	~~sister~~	~~flat~~	bike	mobile
aunt	brother	house	~~car~~	~~computer~~

Sam ____________ a brother, but ____________ an aunt.

Ken ____________, but ____________.

The Bensons ____________. They ____________.

Emma ____________. She ____________.

Alice ____________, but she ____________.

145 ★★☆ Ich möchte alles wissen ...

Stelle Fragen und antworte.

a) ____________ you ____________ a sister, Sam?

No, I ____________ a sister, but I ____________ an aunt.

b) ____________ you ____________ a sister, Ken?

No, I ____________ a sister, but ____________ a brother.

c) ____________ a flat, Mr and Mrs Benson?

No, we ____________ a flat. We ____________ a house.

d) ____________ Emma ____________ a bike?

Yes, ____________ a bike, but she ____________

a car.

144 Sam hasn't got a brother, but he's got an aunt.; Ken hasn't got a sister, but he's got a brother.; The Bensons haven't got a flat. They've got a house.; Emma has got a bike. She hasn't got a car.; Alice has got a mobile phone, but she hasn't got a computer.

145 a) Have you got a sister, Sam? No, I haven't got a sister, but I've got an aunt.; **b)** Have you got a sister, Ken? No, I haven't got a sister, but I've got a brother.; **c)** Have you got a flat, Mr and Mrs Benson? No, we haven't got a flat. We've got a house.; **d)** Has Emma got a bike? Yes, she has got a bike, but she hasn't got a car.

146 ★★☆ Und noch einmal

Schaue dir den Kurztest 144 noch einmal an und gib dann die richtigen Kurzantworten.

Have you got a brother, Sam? ____________________

Has Sam got an aunt? ____________________

Has Ken got a brother? ____________________

Have Mr and Mrs Benson got a house? ____________________

Have you got a flat, Mr and Mrs Benson? ____________________

Has Emma got a bike? ____________________

147 ★★☆ Und wie steht es mit dir?

Gib Kurzantworten.

1. Have you got a sister? ____________________
2. Has your mother got a CD player? ____________________
3. Has she got many CDs? ____________________
4. Have your parents got a computer? ____________________
5. Have you got a mobile phone? ____________________
6. Have your friends got a mobile? ____________________
7. Have you got a pet? ____________________
8. Has it got a cage? ____________________
9. Has your mother got a car? ____________________
10. Has she got an iPod? ____________________
11. Have you and your family got a house? ____________________

146 No, I haven't.; Yes, he has.; Yes, they have.; No, we haven't.; Yes, she has.

147 Mögliche Antworten: **1.** Yes, I have. / No, I haven't.; **2.** Yes, she has. / No, she hasn't.; **3.** Yes, she has. / No, she hasn't.; **4.** Yes, they have. / No, they haven't.; **5.** Yes, I have. / No, I haven't.; **6.** Yes, they have. / No, they haven't.; **7.** Yes, I have. / No, I haven't.; **8.** Yes, it has. / No, it hasn't.; **9.** Yes, she has. / No, she hasn't.; **10.** Yes, she has. / No, she hasn't.; **11.** Yes, we have. / No, we haven't.

148 ★★☆ Deine Schule

Gib Kurzantworten mit *to be* und *have got*.

Is your school a big school? ______

Are there many pupils in your class? ______

Have you got any friends in your class? ______

Have you got a boyfriend / girlfriend? ______

What about your teachers? Are they nice? ______

Have your teachers got time for you? ______

Have you got many lessons in the afternoon? ______

Are you happy with your school reports? ______

Are your parents happy with your school reports? ______

Are you nervous before a test? ______

Is English your favourite subject? ______

149 ★★☆ Pass auf die Schreibung auf!

Wo muss, wo darf kein *e* stehen?

My parents **hav___n't** got a flat. They **hav___** got a house.

Our house **is___n't** a big house, but it is big enough for us.

The rooms **ar___n't** very big, and the garden is small, too.

But I **hav_____** got my own room, and my sister **has___** got her own room, too.

We **ar_____** very happy about that. We **hav______** got enough room for our things.

148 Mögliche Antworten: Yes, it is. / No, it isn't.; Yes, there are. / No, there aren't.; Yes, I have. / No, I haven't.; Yes, I have. / No, I haven't.; Yes, they are. / No, they aren't.; Yes, they have. / No, they haven't.; Yes, I have. / No, I haven't.; Yes, I am. / No, I'm not.; Yes, they are. / No, they aren't.; Yes, I am. / No, I'm not.; Yes, it is. / No, it isn't.

149 haven't; have; isn't; aren't; have; has; are; have.

150 ★★☆ *Can* und *may*

a) Setze die entsprechenden Formen von *can* und *may* ein.

I ______________ speak English, but I ______________ speak Spanish.

______________ we see each other tomorrow, Alice? No, I ______________. I'm busy.

______________ I smoke here, sir? No, you ______________.

______________ I do my homework here? Yes, you ______________.

b) Wo liegen die Unterschiede zwischen *can* und *may*?

____

____

151 ★★☆ Eine Frage in der Not?

Setze die Formen von *can* und *may* ein.

______________ I ask you a question, sir?

Yes, you ______________.

______________ I leave the classroom, sir?

Okay, but first tell me why you want to leave.

I must go to the toilet, sir. ______________ I leave the classroom now?

John, just have a look at your watch. ______________ you tell me the time?

Yes, I ______________. It's three minutes to twelve.

Well, John, then you certainly ______________ wait another three minutes.

Oh sir, I hope I ______________.

150 a) I can speak English, but I can't speak Spanish. Can we see each other tomorrow, Alice? No, I can't. I'm busy. May I smoke here, sir? No, you may not. May I do my homework here? Yes, you may.
b) *can* bedeutet, dass man etwas tun kann oder auch (umgangssprachlich) tun darf. *May* bedeutet ebenfalls „dürfen", ist aber förmlicher als *can*.
151 May I ask you a question, sir? Yes, you may. May I leave the classroom, sir? Okay, but first tell me why you want to leave. I must go to the toilet, sir. May I leave the classroom now? John, just have a look at your watch. Can you tell me the time? Yes, I can. It's three minutes to twelve. Well, John, then you certainly can wait another three minutes. Oh sir, I hope I can.

152 ★★☆ Die Hilfsverben *must / needn't / mustn't*

Übersetze die folgenden Sätze und Fragen.

Muss ich kommen? ______________________________.

Du darfst nicht kommen. ______________________________.

Muss er kommen? ______________________________.

Er muss nicht kommen. ______________________________.

Er braucht nicht zu kommen. ______________________________.

153 ★★☆ Und was sie bedeuten

Setze bitte die entsprechenden Hilfsverben ein.

können	nicht können	dürfen	nicht dürfen	müssen	nicht brauchen / nicht müssen
1.	1.	1.	1.	1.	1.
		2.	2.		
			3.		

154 ★★☆ Was musst du machen, wenn du krank bist?

Stelle dir vor, du wärst krank und müsstest zuhause bleiben. Was dürftest du und was nicht? Setze die richtigen Hilfsverben ein (müssen, dürfen, brauchen).

I ____________ stay in bed.

I ____________ do my homework.

I ____________ play football.

I ____________ take my medicine.

I ____________ go to school.

I ____________ see a doctor.

152 Must I come? You mustn't come. Must he come? He needn't come. He needn't come.
153 können – can; nicht können – can't; dürfen – can / may; nicht dürfen – can't, may not, mustn't; müssen – must; nicht müssen, nicht brauchen – needn't
154 I must stay in bed. I must take my medicine. I needn't do my homework. I needn't go to school. I mustn't play football. I must see a doctor.

155 ★★☆ Was musst, kannst, darfst du (nicht) an der Schule tun?

Setze die richtigen Hilfsverben ein. Es gibt mehrere Möglichkeiten.

I ____________ clean the classroom.

I ____________ kiss my teacher.

I ____________ talk to my neighbour.

I ____________ smoke at school.

I ____________ call my teacher names.

I ____________ listen to my teacher.

I ____________ do my homework.

I ____________ fight with my neighbour.

156 ★★☆ Was kann ich für dich tun?

Übersetze die folgenden Sätze. Gib auf die Wortstellung acht!

Was kann ich für dich tun? ____?

Wie kann ich dir helfen? ____?

Warum kannst du mir nicht helfen? ____?

Was musst du tun? ____?

Wohin musst du gehen? ____?

157 ★★☆ Eine Klage

Korrigiere die Wortstellung.

I / always do / must / what others tell me. ____?

Get up early / must / I. ____?

I / the bus / mustn't / miss. ____?

My homework / do / I / must. ____?

I / at school / stay / must / all day long. ____?

155 Mögliche Antworten: I needn't clean the classroom.; I needn't/mustn't kiss my teacher.; I mustn't talk to my neighbour.; I mustn't smoke at school.; I mustn't call my teacher names.; I must listen to my teacher.; I must do my homework.; I mustn't fight with my neighbour.
156 What can I do for you?; How can I help you?; Why can't you help me?; What must you do?; Where must you go?
157 I must always do what others tell me.; I must get up early.; I mustn't miss the bus.; I must do my homework.; I must stay at school all day long.

158 ★★☆ Hausarbeit

Stelle Fragen.

You / must / your mother / help? ________________________________?

When / her / help / you / must? ________________________________?

How long / her / must / help / you? ________________________________?

Why / you / help / her / must? ________________________________?

What / do / you / must? ________________________________?

Clean / you / the bathroom / must? ________________________________?

The cooking / do / you / must / too? ________________________________?

159 ★☆☆ Eine liebe Mutter

Gib Kurzantworten.

Can I watch this film? Yes, ________________________________.

Can I have a party here tomorrow? Yes, ________________________________.

Can I invite all my friends? Yes, ________________________________.

Can we stay up late? Yes, ________________________________.

Can we go to bed after midnight? Yes, ________________________________.

Can you give me some extra pocket money? Yes, ________________________________.

Can you make us a cake? Yes, ________________________________.

Can I stay home from school the next day? No, ________________________________.

Can I borrow* your CD player? Yes, ________________________________.

Can we smoke in the living room? No, ________________________________.

* to borrow something from someone = sich von jemandem etwas ausleihen

158 Must you help your mother?; When must you help her?; How long must you help her?; Why must you help her?; What must you do?; Must you clean the bathroom?; Must you do the cooking, too?
159 Yes, you can.; Yes, you can.; Yes, you can.; Yes, you can.; Yes, you can.; Yes, I can.; Yes, I can.; No, you cannot/ can't.; Yes, you can.; No, you can't.

160 ★☆☆ Aufforderungen

Übersetze diese Sätze.

Come here, Tom. ________________

Come here, Tom and Mike. ________________

Come here, Mr Benson. ________________

Come over to our place, Mrs Benson. ________________

Come with us, Mr and Mrs Benson. ________________

161 ★★☆ Was du so zu Hause hörst ...

Welche Verben könntest du hier einsetzen?

C ________________ back soon.

B ________________ here at seven.

P ________________ up your socks.

E ________________ your soup.

T ________________ up your room.

H ________________ a bath or a shower.

W ________________ your hands.

B ________________ your teeth.

D ________________ your homework.

H ________________ me now.

S ________________ the table.

D ________________ the dishes.

G ________________ to bed now.

160 Komm ..., Kommt ..., Kommen Sie ..., Kommen Sie ..., Kommen Sie ...

161 Come back soon.; Be here at seven.; Pull/Pick up your socks.; Eat up your soup.; Tidy up your room.; Have a bath or a shower.; Wash your hands.; Brush your teeth.; Do your homework.; Help me now.; Set the table.; Do the dishes.; Go to bed now.

162 ★★☆ … und in der Schule

Gebrauche verneinte Formen, wo sie sinnvoll sind.

forget your homework ______________________

talk to your neighbour ______________________

listen to me ______________________

fall asleep ______________________

speak German in English lessons ______________________

kick your neighbour ______________________

leave him alone ______________________

run around in the classroom ______________________

be late ______________________

do your homework now, do it later ______________________

be so loud ______________________

163 ★★☆ Augen auf im Straßenverkehr

Wandle die folgenden Sätze um. Gebrauche Imperative.

You must watch out for cars. ______________________

You must stop at red traffic lights. ______________________

You mustn't cross the street when the lights are red. ______________________

You mustn't play football in a busy street. ______________________

You mustn't ride your bike on the pavement. ______________________

You mustn't hurt anybody. ______________________

You mustn't stop in the middle of the street. ______________________

162 Don't forget your homework.; Don't talk to your neighbour.; Listen to me.; Don't fall asleep.; Don't speak German in English lessons.; Don't kick your neighbour.; Leave him alone.; Don't run around in the classroom.; Don't be late.; Don't do your homework now, do it later.; Don't be so loud.

163 Watch out for cars.; Stop at red traffic lights.; Don't cross the street when the lights are red.; Don't play football in a busy street.; Don't ride your bike on the pavement.; Don't hurt anybody.; Don't stop in the middle of the street.

164 ★☆☆ Die regelmäßige Bildung des Partizip Präsens

Bilde das Partizip Präsens der folgenden Verben.

clean ______	wash ______	sing ______
laugh ______	talk ______	fight ______
drink ______	eat ______	listen ______
shout ______	knock ______	do ______
watch ______	fix ______	go ______
buy ______	play ______	say ______
cry ______	try ______	carry ______

165 ★★☆ Etwas weniger regelmäßige Formen ...

Beachte die Bildung des Partizip Präsens bei den folgenden Verben.

write ______	choose ______	lose ______
come ______	ride ______	take ______
change ______	have ______	drive ______
trip ______	plan ______	put ______
sit ______	clap ______	run ______
drop ______	stop ______	swim ______
cut ______	get ______	forget ______
lie ______	die ______	tie ______

164 cleaning, laughing, drinking, shouting, watching, buying, crying; washing, talking, eating, knocking, fixing, playing, trying; singing , fighting, listening, doing, going, saying, carrying.

165 writing, coming, changing, tripping, sitting, dropping, cutting, lying; choosing, riding, having, planning, clapping, stopping, getting, dying; losing, taking, driving, putting, running, swimming, forgetting, tying

166 ★★☆ In der Pause

Was machen die Kinder gerade im Pausenhof? Bilde Sätze mit den folgenden Angaben.

They / eat their sandwiches ______________________

Many / stand together in groups ______________________

They / talk ______________________

Somebody / shout ______________________

Some children / play ______________________

Two pupils / fight ______________________

Somebody / call a teacher ______________________

167 ★★☆ Nach der Pause

Bilde Sätze im *present progressive*.

The pupils / leave the schoolyard. ______________________

They / go into the school building. ______________________

Some / run. ______________________

A pupil / lie / on the floor. ______________________

He / cry. ______________________

A teacher / come. ______________________

The teacher / carry him into the office. ______________________

He put / him on a stretcher*. ______________________

The secretary / get him a glass of water. ______________________

She / call an ambulance. ______________________

* stretcher = Bahre

166 They are eating their sandwiches.; They are standing together in groups.; They are talking.; Somebody is shouting.; Some children are playing.; Two pupils are fighting.; Somebody is calling a teacher.

167 The pupils are leaving the schoolyard.; They are going into the school building.; Some are running.; A pupil is lying on the floor.; He is crying.; A teacher is coming.; The teacher is carrying him into the office.; He is putting him on a stretcher.; The secretary is getting him a glass of water.; She is calling an ambulance.

168 ★★☆ Was weißt du noch?

Lies die Regeln und fülle die Lücken aus.

a) Das present progressive besteht immer aus zwei Teilen:

(1) aus einer Form von *to be* und (2) aus dem *Partizip Präsens*.

Shh! Be quiet! We ____________ (to be) ____________________ (listen) to the teacher!

b) Das Partizip des Präsens bildest du, indem du *-ing* an den Infinitiv ohne *to* anhängst:

to go = __________________, to do = __________________, to try = __________________

c) Bei vielen einsilbigen Verben, die auf einen Konsonant enden, wird der Konsonant verdoppelt. Bei Verben wie *to take*, die auf ein -*e* enden, das nicht ausgesprochen wird, entfällt das -*e*. Bei Verben, die wie *to lie* auf -*ie* enden, wird das -*ie* zu -*y*:

to stop = __________________, to take = __________________, to die = __________________

169 ★★☆ Der Anfang einer Englischstunde

Die Schüler sind wieder im Klassenzimmer, aber ihr Lehrer ist noch nicht da.
Schreibe auf, was sie nicht tun.

The pupils (not sit) in their chairs. ________________________________

They (not do) their exercises. ________________________________

They (not take) notes. ________________________________

They (not look) at their exercise books. ________________________________

They (not work). ________________________________

Tom (not sleep). ________________________________

Mike (not flirt) with Alice. ________________________________

Alice (not write) letters to her neighbours. ________________________________

Kevin and Ken (not throw) things at the girls. ________________________________

168 a) Shh! Be quiet! We are listening to the teacher! **b)** going, doing, trying **c)** stopping, taking, dying.

169 The pupils aren't sitting in their chairs.; They are not doing their exercises.; They aren't taking notes.; They aren't looking at their exercise books.; They aren't working.; Tom isn't sleeping.; Mike isn't flirting with Alice.; Alice isn't writing letters to her neighbours.; Kevin and Ken aren't throwing things at the girls.

170 ★★☆ Der Lehrer kommt ...

Was tun sie gerade? Bilde Fragen.

Tom / sit / in* his chair? ______________________________?

He / do / an exercise? ______________________________?

Kevin and Ken / make / girls angry? ______________________________?

Alice / flirt / with Mike? ______________________________?

Robert / lie / on the floor? ______________________________?

Bob, Ben and John / play / cards? ______________________________?

Debbie / read / a magazine? ______________________________?

Fiona / run / around the classroom? ______________________________?

Tim / play / football in the classroom? ______________________________?

* Man kann sowohl *to sit in a chair* als auch *to sit on a chair* sagen. Beides ist richtig.

171 ★★☆ Ja oder nein?

Schaue dir den vorigen Kurztest noch einmal an und gib dann Kurzantworten.

Is Debbie reading a magazine? Yes, ______________________________.

Is Robert running around the classroom? No, ______________________________.

Are Kevin and Ken doing exercises? No, ______________________________.

Is Alice flirting with Tom? No, ______________________________.

Are Fiona and Tom playing cards? No, ______________________________.

Is Tom doing his exercises? Yes, ______________________________.

Is Ben lying on the floor? No, ______________________________.

Is Debbie crying? No, ______________________________.

Are Kevin and Ken playing with the girls? No, ______________________________.

Is Tim drawing a picture? No, ______________________________.

170 Is Tom sitting in his chair?; Is he doing an exercise?; Are Kevin and Ken making the girls angry?; Is Alice flirting with Mike?; Is Robert lying on the floor?; Are Bob, Ben and John playing cards?; Is Debbie reading a magazine?; Is Fiona running around the classroom?; Is Tim playing football in the classroom?
171 Yes, she is.; No, he isn't.; No, they aren't.; No, she isn't.; No, they aren't.; Yes, he is.; No, he isn't.; No, she isn't.; No, they aren't.; No, he isn't.

172 ★★☆ Wie sieht es aus, wenn der Lehrer zu spät kommt?

Gib Kurzantworten.

Are you all sitting on your chairs? ______________________

Are you running around the classroom? ______________________

Are you still doing your homework? ______________________

Are you playing cards? ______________________

And what about the others?

Are they all waiting for their teacher? ______________________

Are they leaving the classroom? ______________________

Are they drawing pictures on the board? ______________________

173 ★★☆ Lehrerfragen

Stelle Fragen mit Fragewörtern.

Where you / go? ______________________ ?

What you / do? ______________________ ?

Why / you / not listen? ______________________ ?

Who / talk? ______________________ ?

What / you / read? ______________________ ?

Why / you / leave the room? ______________________ ?

Why you / not take notes? ______________________ ?

Why / you / not / do this exercise? ______________________ ?

172 Mögliche Antworten: Yes, we are. / No, we aren't.; Yes, we are. / No, we aren't.; Yes, we are. / No, we aren't.; Yes, we are. / No, we aren't.; Yes, they are. / No, they aren't.; Yes, they are. / No, they aren't.; Yes, they are. / No, they aren't.

173 Where are you going?; What are you doing?; Why are you not listening? / Why aren't you listening?; Who is talking?; What are you reading?; Why are you leaving the room?; Why are you not taking notes? / Why aren't you taking notes?; Why aren't you doing this exercise? / Why are you not doing this exercise?

174 ★★★ Verben mit Präpositionen

Füge die entsprechende Präposition hinzu.

What are you looking ____________________ ? (suchen)

Who are you waiting ____________________ ? (warten)

Who are you looking ____________________ ? (ansehen)

What are you listening ____________________ ? (zuhören)

What are you talking ____________________ ? (reden über)

Who are you looking ____________________ ? (sich kümmern um)

Who are you thinking ____________________ ? (denken an)

Why are you running ____________________ ? (wegrennen)

What are you writing ____________________ ? (aufschreiben)

What word are you looking ____________________ ? (nachschlagen)

What are you putting ____________________ your bag? (hineintun)

What trousers are you trying ____________________ ? (anprobieren)

175 ★★★ Was ist das Gegenteil?

Setze die richtige Präposition ein.

to get on a bus	to get ____________________ a bus
to turn a radio on	to turn it ____________________
to put on a shirt	to take it ____________________
to take off your clothes	to put them ____________________
to fall asleep	to wake ____________________
to stand up	to sit ____________________

174 What are you looking for?; Who are you waiting for?; Who are you looking at?; What are you listening to?; What are you talking about?; Who are you looking after?; Who are you thinking of? (*think of = denken an; think about = nachdenken über*); Why are you running away?; What are you writing down?; What word are you looking up?; What are you putting in your bag?; What trousers are you trying on?
175 to get off a bus, to turn it off, to take it off, to put them on, to wake up, to sit down

176 ★☆☆ Bejahte Formen

a) Setze die dritte Person Singular ein.

he ______________________ (play) she ______________________ (do)

he ______________________ (carry) she ______________________ (watch)

she ______________________ (go) he ______________________ (die)

he ______________________ (say) she ______________________ (kiss)

he ______________________ (try) she ______________________ (have)

he ______________________ (buy) she ______________________ (make)

b) Unterstreiche die Verben, die unregelmäßig sind und schreibe sie heraus.

______________________ ______________________

______________________ ______________________

177 ★★☆ Ein Morgen in Toms Leben

Setze die 3. Person Singular ein.

His mother ____________ him up at seven. (wake)

He ____________ to wake up. (try)

He ______________, then he ________________. (wash / get dressed)

After that he __________ breakfast. (have)

He ________ goodbye to his mother. (say)

Then he __________ his things and __________ the house. (pack / leave)

He __________ to the bus station and __________ the bus. (go / catch)

Sometimes he __________ his homework on the bus. (do)

At half past eight he ________ at school. (arrive)

176 a) plays, carries, goes, says, tries, buys; does, watches, dies, kisses, has, makes
b) to do, to go, to have, to say (nur in der Aussprache)
177 His mother wakes him up at seven.; He tries to wake up.; He washes, then he gets dressed.; After that he has breakfast.; He says goodbye to his mother.; Then he packs his things and leaves the house.; He goes to the bus station and catches the bus.; Sometimes he does his homework on the bus.; At half past eight he arrives at school.

178 ★★☆ Ein typischer Abend bei den Bensons

Setze die richtigen Verbformen ein.

When the Bensons __________ home, it's still very early.	come
Then they __________ tea.	have
After tea, they __________ up the dishes.	wash
Tom sometimes __________ them.	help
Then Mrs Benson __________ his newspaper.	read
Mrs Benson __________ a magazine or a book.	read
Later they __________ TV.	watch
Mr Benson __________ films. His wife __________ so, too.	like / do
At about eleven they __________ to bed.	go

179 ★★☆ Und was tun sie *nicht* am Wochende?

Gebrauche die verneinten Formen des *simple present*.

The Bensons / not get up / early.	They __________________.
Mrs Benson / not go / to work.	She __________________
They / not have / an early breakfast.	They __________________
They / not make / their beds.	They __________________
Tom / not do / any homework.	He __________________
He / not go / to school.	He __________________
Mr Benson / not do / the gardening.	He __________________
The Bensons / not stay / at home all day.	They __________________

178 When the Bensons come home …; Then they have tea.; After tea they wash up the dishes.; Tom sometimes helps them.; Then Mr Benson reads his newspaper.; Mrs Benson reads …; Later they watch TV.; Mr Benson likes films. His wife does so, too.; At about eleven they go to bed.

179 … don't get up early.; … doesn't go to work.; … don't have an early breakfast.; … don't make their beds.; … doesn't do any homework.; … doesn't go to school.; … doesn't do the gardening.; … don't stay at home all day.

180 ★★☆ Und was tust du an Sonntagen?

Gebrauche verneinte Formen bei den Sätzen, die für dich nicht zutreffen.

On Sundays

I learn English. ____________________.

I listen to music. ____________________.

I go for a walk with my girlfriend / boyfriend. ____________________.

I clean the windows in my room. ____________________.

I write e-mails to my friends. ____________________.

I make breakfast for my parents. ____________________.

I go to school. ____________________.

I watch TV. ____________________.

181 ★★☆ Ein Interview

Frage deinen Lehrer / deine Lehrerin, was er / sie am Wochenende normalerweise macht. Benutze dabei die folgenden Verben bzw. Angaben.

go out in the evening ____________________.

correct tests ____________________.

get up late ____________________.

stay in bed all day ____________________.

play computer games ____________________.

go shopping ____________________.

visit your parents ____________________.

call your students' parents ____________________.

go to the park with your family ____________________.

180 Mögliche Antworten: On Sundays, I learn / don't learn English.; I listen / don't listen to music.; I go / don't go for a walk with my girlfriend / boyfriend.; I clean / don't clean the windows in my room.; I write / don't write emails to my friends.; I make / don't make breakfast for my parents.; I go / don't go to school.; I watch / don't watch TV.

181 Do you go out in the evening?; Do you correct tests?; Do you get up late?; Do you stay in bed all day?; Do you play computer games?; Do you go shopping?; Do you visit your parents?; Do you call your students' parents?; Do you go to the park with your family?

182 ★★☆ Vorlieben und Abneigungen

Gib Kurzantworten.

Do you like pets? Yes / No, ______

Do you like sports? ______

Do your parents like sports? ______

Does your father play football? ______

Does he watch football on TV? ______

Does your mother like boxing? ______

Do your parents smoke? ______

Do people like you? ______

Do your teachers like you? ______

Do you hate English? ______

183 ★★☆ Was bist du für ein Mensch?

Gib Kurzantworten.

Do you like people? ______

Are you afraid of people? ______

Are people afraid of you? ______

Do you often go out alone? ______

Have you got any friends? ______

Do you help other people? ______

Do people help you? ______

Are you laughing now? ______

182 Yes, I do. / No, I don't.; Yes, I do. / No, I don't.; Yes, they do. / No, they don't.; Yes, he does. / No, he doesn't.; Yes, he does / No, he doesn't.; Yes, she does. / No, she doesn't.; Yes, they do. / No, they don't.; Yes, they do. / No, they don't.; Yes, they do. / No, they don't.; Yes, I do. / No, I don't.

183 Yes, I do. / No, I don't.; Yes, I am. / No, I'm not.; Yes, they are. / No, they aren't.; Yes, I do. / No, I don't.; Yes, I have. / No, I haven't.; Yes, I do. / No, I don't.; Yes, they do. / No, they don't.; Yes, I am. / No, I'm not.

184 ★★☆ Einige Fragewörter

Mit welchen Fragewörtern fragst du nach dem Subjekt, Objekt usw.? Trage sie in die Tabelle ein.

Debbie	sees	Tom	in the classroom	at 9.
The shop	shows	its top cars	in its showrooms	this week.
Subjekt	**Verb**	**Objekt**	**Ort**	**Zeit**
a) ______ b) ______	______	a) ______ b) ______	______	______

185 ★★☆ Fragen im *simple present*

Frage nach dem Subjekt, dem Verb, dem Objekt, dem Ort und der Zeit in den oben stehenden Sätzen.

a) Subjekt: ______________________

____

b) Verb: ______________________

____

c) Objekt: ______________________

____

d) Ort: ______________________

____

e) Zeit: ______________________

____

184 Subjekt: **a), b)** *who / what*; Verb: *what*; Objekt: **a), b)** *who / what*; Ort: *where*; Zeit: *when*
185 a) Who sees Tom …? What shows its top cars …? **b)** What does Debbie do …? What does the shop do …? **c)** Who does Debbie see …? What does the shop show …? **d)** Where does Debbie see Tom at 9? Where does the shop show its top cars this week? **e)** When does Debbie see Tom in the classroom? When does the shop show its top cars?

186 ★★☆ Die Fragebildung

Schaue dir die Fragen aus dem vorigen Kurztest noch einmal genau an und vergleiche sie mit der Lösung. Beantworte dann die folgenden Fragen.

a) Wann musst du *what*, wann *who* gebrauchen?

what: ● Sachen ● Personen ● Zeiten

who: ● Sachen ● Personen ● Orte

b) Welches Fragewort musst du gebrauchen, wenn du nach dem Verb fragst?

● how ● who ● when ● why ● what ● where

c) Wann gebrauchst du *to do* bei der Fragebildung nicht?

● in Fragen nach dem Objekt ● in Fragen nach dem Verb

● in positiven Fragen nach dem Subjekt

d) Bei einer Frage nach dem Subjekt steht das Verb im Plural oder im Singular?
Kleiner Tipp: Im Deutschen ist es genauso!

● Im Singular ● Im Plural

187 ★★☆ Mr Hedges

Stelle jeweils zwei Fragen nach den hervorgehobenen Satzteilen.

Mr Hedges works as a caretaker **at Tom's school.**

____?

____?

He likes **his job.**

____?

____?

Children like **him.**

____?

____?

186 a) what für Sachen, who für Personen; **b)** what; **c)** nicht bei positiven Fragen nach dem Subjekt; **d)** Im Singular
187 Who works as a caretaker at Tom's school? Where does Mr Hedges work? Who likes his job? What does he like? Who likes him? Who do children like?

188 ★★☆ Ein Nachmittag

Stelle Fragen nach den hervorgehobenen Satzteilen.

a) **Mr Mason** is a teacher.
b) Mr Mason is **at home**.
c) He **corrects** his pupils' tests at home.
d) He always corrects them **on Saturday afternoon**.
e) He often finds **a lot of mistakes** in their tests.
f) He doesn't always like **what he sees**.
g) Sometimes **he** gets angry.

a) ______________________________?

b) ______________________________?

c) ______________________________?

d) ______________________________?

e) ______________________________?

f) ______________________________?

g) ______________________________?

189 ★★☆ Ein bitterer Nachmittag

Stelle Fragen nach den hervorgehobenen Satzteilen.

a) He **gives** his pupils a lot of work.

____

b) He calls **his wife**.

____

c) He corrects **the mistakes**.

____

d) **Mr Mason** begins to cry when he sees the pupils' mistakes.

____

188 a) Who is Mr Mason? **b)** Where is Mr Mason? **c)** What is he doing? **d)** When does he correct them? **e)** What does he often find in their tests? **f)** What doesn't he always like? **g)** Who gets angry sometimes?
189 a) What does he do? **b)** Who does he call? **c)** What does he correct? **d)** Who begins to cry?

190 ★★☆ Weitere Fragewörter

Setze *how, why, which, what* ein.

__________ many books do you read a year? About 50 books, I think.

__________ often do you go to the public library? Once a week.

__________ don't you buy them? They are too expensive.

__________ much does this book cost? It costs £10.

__________ book are you talking about? The green book over there.

__________ do you read so many books? I like books.

__________ kind of books do you like? I like all kinds of books.

191 ★★★ Du und das Fernsehen

Übersetze die folgenden Fragen.

Magst du Fernsehen? __________

Was schaust du normalerweise im Fernsehen an? __________

Was für Filme magst du? __________

Was sagen deine Eltern dazu? __________

Welche anderen Programme schaust du dir an? __________

Wie oft machst du das Fernsehen an? __________

Wie lange schaust du fern? __________

Wann machst du das Fernsehen aus? __________

Schläfst* du manchmal vor dem Fernseher ein? __________

Wann gehst du ins Bett? __________

* to fall asleep = einschlafen

190 how, how, why, how, which, why, what

191 Do you like (watching) TV?; What do you normally watch on TV?; What kind of films do you like?; What do your parents say about them / the films?; What other programmes do you watch?; How often do you turn on the TV?; How long do you watch TV?; When do you turn off the TV?; Do you sometimes fall asleep in front of the TV?; When do you go to bed?

192 ★★☆ Debbies Notizen

Debbie hat sich Notizen über ihren Tagesablauf gemacht. Die Reihenfolge stimmt allerdings nicht. Nummeriere die Sätze in der richtigen Reihenfolge.

- go to bed and read a book
- wake up
- have supper
- leave the house
- wash / dress
- have lunch at school
- kiss her mother goodbye
- come home in the late afternoon
- do homework
- go to her first class, English
- fall asleep
- watch TV
- have breakfast
- run to the bus

193 ★★☆ Debbies Tag

Schreibe auf, was Debbie tut (s. Kurztest Nr. 192) und verbinde die einzelnen Sätze mit den folgenden Signalwörtern:

afterwards *first* *then* *the next day* *after that* *after* *before*

First she ______________________________

192 1. wake up; **2.** wash / dress; **3.** have breakfast; **4.** kiss her mother goodbye; **5.** leave the house; **6.** run to the bus; **7.** go to her first class, English; **8.** have lunch at school; **9.** come home in the late afternoon; **10.** do her homework; **11.** have supper; **12.** watch TV; **13.** go to bed and read a book; **14.** fall asleep

193 Mögliche Antworten: First Debbie wakes up, then she washes, dresses and has breakfast. After that she goes to school. She kisses her mother good-bye, then she runs to the bus. When the morning lessons are over, she has lunch at school, too. After she comes home in the late afternoon, she does her homework. Afterwards she has supper. Then she watches TV or plays a game or two. After that she goes to bed and reads a book. The next day she goes to school again.

194 ★★☆ Wie sieht es bei den Bensons aus?

Schreibe, wie der Tag bei den Bensons verläuft. Gebrauche die folgenden Angaben. Die Verben und Signalwörter musst du allerdings ergänzen.

get up at seven / wash / dress / breakfast / leave the house at 8 / Mrs Benson bus / work in a hospital / look after patients / lunch there, too / Mr Benson work for a newspaper / write and correct articles / often Mr Benson lunch in town / the Bensons home in the early evening / tea or supper

195 ★★☆ Und was tun sie am Abend?

Übersetze die hervorgehobenen Signalwörter für das *simple present*.

They **often** play with their children.

They **always** talk to them.

They **often** help them with their homework.

They **usually** watch TV or read a book.

They **sometimes** go out.

They **never** stay out all night.

Sometimes their friends come to see them.

They **always** have a good time.

They are **seldom** bored.

They **never** get angry.

194 The Bensons get up at seven. They wash and dress. Then they have breakfast. At 8 they leave the house. Mrs Benson takes the bus. She works in a hospital. She looks after patients. She has lunch there, too. Mr Benson works for a newspaper. He writes and corrects articles. He often has lunch in town. The Bensons come home in the early evening. Then they have tea or supper.

195 oft, immer, oft, gewöhnlich / normalerweise, manchmal, nie/niemals, manchmal, immer, selten, nie.

196 ★★☆ Was weißt du noch?

Sieh dir den Kurztest Nr. 195 nochmals an und kreuze dann die richtigen Antworten an.

1. Wo stehen die Signalwörter bei den einfachen Formen von *to be*?
   - vor dem Verb
   - hinter dem Verb
2. Wo stehen die Signalwörter bei dem *simple present*?
   - vor dem Verb
   - hinter dem Verb?
3. Wo stehen die Signalwörter bei verneinten Formen des *simple present*?
   - vor dem Verb
   - hinter dem Verb
4. Wo kann *sometimes* noch stehen?
   - überall
   - am Satzanfang

197 ★★☆ Ein Musterschüler

Setze die Signalwörter ein.

He forgets his homework. ______________________ (nie)

He is late. ______________________ (niemals)

He is on time. ______________________ (immer)

He listens to his teacher. ______________________ (immer)

He doesn't talk in class. ______________________ (immer)

He is bored. ______________________ (niemals)

He knows everything. ______________________ (gewöhnlich)

He forgets things. ______________________ (selten)

We make fun of him. ______________________ (manchmal)

But it's not funny! ______________________ (manchmal)

196 **1.** Hinter dem Verb, **2.** Vor dem Verb, **3.** Vor dem Verb, **4.** Am Satzanfang
197 He never forgets his homework.; He is never late.; He is always on time.; He always listens to his teacher.; He doesn't always talk in class.; He is never bored.; He usually knows everything.; He seldom forgets things.; We sometimes make fun of him.; But sometimes it's not funny.

198 ★★☆ Ein richtiger Engel

Beantworte die folgenden Fragen mit einer Kurzantwort und Signalwörtern wie *never, always* etc.

1. Do you often drive your teachers crazy? (No / never)

   ____

2. Are you always a friendly person? (Yes / seldom unfriendly)

   ____

3. Are you always happy when you go to school? (Yes / always)

   ____

4. Do your teachers give you good marks*? (Yes / usually)

   ____

5. Do you listen to your teachers? (Yes / always)

   ____

* marks (AmE: grades) = Noten (Schule)

199 ★★☆ Und was tust du sonst noch?

Schreibe auf, was du tust. Verwende die folgenden Angaben und Signalwörter:

play computer games with my friends *get older* *get a birthday present*
get pocket money from my parents *brush my teeth*

Every morning I ______________________________.

Every afternoon I ______________________________.

Every day I ______________________________.

Every week I ______________________________.

Every year I ______________________________.

198 1. No, I don't. I never drive my teachers crazy. **2.** Yes, I am. I am seldom unfriendly. **3.** Yes, I am. I'm always happy when I go to school. **4.** Yes, they do. They usually give me good marks. **5.** Yes, I do. I always listen to them.
199 Mögliche Antworten: Every morning I brush my teeth. Every afternoon I play computer games with friends. Every day I get older. Every week I get pocket money from my parents. Every year I get a birthday present.

200 ★★☆ Und was geschieht gerade jetzt?

a) Bilde Sätze mit den angegebenen Verben.

The sun ______________________________ . (shine)

It's not ______________________________ . (rain)

The birds ______________________________ . (sing)

And we ______________________________ indoors! (sit)

We ______________________________ a test*. (do)

Look! Mike ______________________________ . (dream)

He ______________________________ to the birds. (listen)

Our teacher ______________________________ to talk to Mike. (try)

b) Erkläre, warum du hier das *present progressive* gebrauchen musst.

____

____

* einen Test schreiben = to do a test (AmE: to take a test)

201 ★★☆ Signalwörter

Welche Signalwörter kannst du nicht mit dem *present progressive* gebrauchen?

next year	listen!	this morning	then
at this moment	just	this afternoon	today
look!	now	this evening	the next day
every morning	after that	the next evening	seldom

200 a) The sun is shining.; It's not raining.; The birds are singing.; And we are sitting indoors!; We are doing a test.; Look! Mike is dreaming.; He is listening to the birds.; Our teacher is trying to talk to Mike.
b) Die Handlung läuft gerade ab, ist also noch nicht abgeschlossen.
201 *next year, then, the next day, every morning, after that, the next evening, seldom* sind **keine** Signalwörter für das *present progressive*.

202 ★★☆ David bei der Arbeit

Das *simple present* oder das *present progressive*? Was ist richtig?

Where is David?

He ______________________ (clean) Debbie's bike.

What? Why ________ he _____________ (clean) her bike during my English lesson?

That ___________ (be) his birthday present to her.

Okay, okay, I ___________ (see). He ____________ (know) we have English today, doesn't he?

I ______________________ (think) so.

Well, maybe he _____________________ (not know) that it's my birthday, too. He can clean my car too – as a birthday present to me!

203 ★★☆ Fragen und Antworten

Das *simple present* oder das *present progressive*? Beantworte die Fragen.

a) Doesn't Mr Brown live here? No, he doesn't. He ____________ in London now. (live)

b) Can I talk to Debbie? I'm afraid not*. She ____________________ a bath. (have)

c) Can you talk to me, Bob? Sorry, not now, I __________________ the football match on TV. (watch)

d) Look! That's Bobby's team. They ________________ against another school. (play)

________ you _______ football, too? (play)

e) Tom, where are you? In my room. What _________ you __________ there? (do)

I _____________ very busy (be). I _________________ my homework. (do)

* I'm afraid not. = Leider nicht.

202 … He is cleaning Debbie's bike. What? Why is he cleaning her bike during my English lesson? That is his birthday present to her. Okay, okay, I see. He knows we have English today, doesn't he? I think so. Well, maybe he doesn't know that …

203 a) He lives in London now. **b)** She is having a bath. **c)** I'm watching the football match on TV. **d)** They are playing against another school. Do you play football, too? **e)** What are you doing there? I'm very busy. I'm doing my homework.

204 ★★☆ Ein armes Mädchen

Welche der hervorgehobenen Verben kannst du normalerweise nicht im *present progressive* verwenden? Unterstreiche sie.

Everybody **knows** me, but nobody **understands** me.

Nobody **comes** to see me. Nobody **talks** to me. I **am** all alone.

Nobody **likes** me, nobody **wants me** and nobody **loves** me. I **cry** all day.

Can you **hear** me? Can you **see** me?

205 ★★★ Ein „böses" Mädchen

***Present progressive* oder *simple present*?**

Alice often __________ TV, but this evening she __________ to watch anything. (watch / not want)

She __________ to go out. Today __________ her girlfriend's birthday, and there will be a party at her house. (want / be)

Alice __________ to be there, but her mother __________ her friends. (want / not like)

She __________ why Alice __________ such friends. (not understand / have)

What can Alice do? Look! She __________ (be) in her room.

She __________ in front of the mirror. She __________ on her new dress and a bit of make-up! (stand / put)

What __________ she __________?! (do) She __________ out. (go)

__________ she always __________ things like that? (do)

Yes. She always __________ what she wants! (do)

204 know, understand, be, like, want, love, hear, see

205 Alice often watches TV, but this evening she doesn't want to watch anything. She wants to go out. Today is her girlfriend's birthday, and there will be a party at her house. Alice wants to be there, but her mother doesn't like her friends. She doesn't understand why Alice has such friends. What can Alice do? Look! She is in her room. She is standing in front of the mirror. She is putting on her new dress and a bit of make-up! What is she doing?! She is going out. Does she always do things like that? Yes, she always does what she wants!

206 ★☆☆ Tom war krank

Setze die Formen des *simple past* von *to be* ein.

a) Last week Tom ________________ ill.

b) He ________________ at home.

c) His parents ________________ also at home.

d) His friends ________________ there, too.

e) I ________________ there, too.

f) The room ________________ full of people.

g) There ________________ very little room in front of his bed.

h) Everybody ________________ worried.

i) Only Tom ________________ happy.

j) He ________________ not at school, and he missed the English exam!

207 ★☆☆ Tom ist immer noch krank

Setze die verneinten Vergangenheitsformen von *to be* ein.

Tom ________________ well.

His friends ________________ happy.

You ________________ happy.

His mother ________________ happy either.

His parents called the doctor, but he ________________ there.

He ________________ at home.

We ________________ happy about that.

206 a) Last week Tom was ill. **b)** He was at home. **c)** His parents were also at home. **d)** His friends were there, too. **e)** I was there, too. **f)** The room was full of people. **g)** There was very little room in front of his bed. **h)** Everybody was worried. **i)** Only Tom was happy. **j)** He was not at school …
207 Tom wasn't well. His friends weren't happy. You weren't happy. His mother wasn't happy either. His parents called the doctor, but he wasn't there. He wasn't at home. We weren't happy about that.

208 ★☆☆ Lang- und Kurzformen von *to be* im *simple past*

Ergänze die fehlenden Formen.

I	was	not	I ____________
you	____________	not	you ____________
he, she, it	____________	not	he, she, it ____________
we	____________	not	we ____________
you	____________	not	you ____________
they	____________	not	they ____________

209 ★☆☆ Fragen mit dem *past* von *to be*

Schaue dir den Kurztest 206 noch einmal an und stelle dann die entsprechenden Fragen.

a) ____ ?

b) ____ ?

c) ____ ?

d) ____ ?

e) ____ ?

f) ____ ?

g) ____ ?

h) ____ ?

i) ____ ?

j) ____ ?

208 I was not; you were not; he, she, it was not; we were not; you were not; they were not; I wasn't; you weren't; he, she, it wasn't; we weren't; you weren't; they weren't.
209 a) Was Tom ill last week? **b)** Was he at home? **c)** Were his parents at home, too? **d)** Were his friends there, too. **e)** Was I / were you there, too? **f)** Was the room full of people? **g)** Was there little room in front of his bed? **h)** Was everybody worried? **i)** Was Tom happy? **j)** Was he at school?

210 ★★☆ Fragen an Tom

Setze die Formen des *simple past* von *to be* ein und gib Kurzantworten.

a) ____________ you ill, Tom? Yes, ____________________.

b) ____________ you worried? No, ____________________.

c) ____________ your parents worried? Yes, ____________________.

d) ____________ your friends there? Yes, ____________________.

e) ____________ all of them there? No, ____________________.

f) ____________ Alice there? No, ____________________.

g) ____________ Debbie there? Yes, ____________________.

h) ____________ she rude to you? No, ____________________.

i) ____________ you happy? Yes, ____________________.

211 ★★☆ Weitere Fragen an Tom

Stelle Fragen mit Fragewörtern. Ergänze die fehlenden Formen von *to be*.

Why / not at school last week? ____________________?

How long / ill? ____________________?

Why / ill? ____________________?

When / better again? ____________________?

How many of your friends / there? ____________________?

Who / missing? ____________________?

Why / Debbie not there? ____________________?

Where / the doctor? ____________________?

210 a) Were … / Yes, I was. **b)** Were … / No, I wasn't. **c)** Were … / Yes, they were. **d)** Were … / Yes, they were. **e)** Were … / No, they weren't. **f)** Was … / No, she wasn't. **g)** Was … / Yes, she was. **h)** Was / No, she wasn't. **i)** Were / Yes, I was.

211 Why were you not at school last week? How long were you ill? Why were you ill? When were you better again? How many of your friends were there? Who was missing? Why was Debbie not there? Where was the doctor?

212 ★★☆ Das *past progressive*

a) Wie wird das *present progressive* gebildet?

Mit dem
- Präsens von *to be*
- Präsens von *to do*

und dem
- Partizip Präsens
- Partizip Perfekt

b) Und wie steht es mit dem *past progressive*? Es wird gebildet

mit der
- Vergangenheit von *to be*
- Vergangenheit von *to do*

und dem
- Partizip Perfekt
- Partizip Präsens

c) Vervollständige die folgenden Sätze:

What ________ you ________ (do) right now?

What ________ you ________ (do) yesterday when I called you?

213 ★☆☆ Das Partizip Präsens

Bilde das Partizip Präsens der folgenden Verben.

watch ________

make ________

sit ________

go ________

lie ________

swim ________

play ________

carry ________

fetch ________

take ________

run ________

do ________

die ________

cry ________

try ________

hurry ________

212 a) Mit dem Präsens von **to be** und dem Partizip Präsens; **b)** mit der Vergangenheit von **to be** und dem Partizip Präsens; **c)** What are you doing right now? What were you doing yesterday when I called you?

213 watching, making, sitting, going, lying, swimming, playing, carrying; fetching, taking, running, doing, dying, crying, trying, hurrying

214 ★★☆ Gestern um 7 Uhr …

Bilde Sätze mit dem *past progressive*.

When the doorbell rang yesterday morning at seven o'clock, …

I / just get up ______________________________

my parents / have breakfast ______________________________

my father / read morning paper ______________________________

my sister / still sleep ______________________________

our neighbors / still lie in their beds ______________________________

my younger brother / still dream ______________________________

other people / have a good time ______________________________

215 ★★☆ Gestern um 11 Uhr morgens

Bilde Sätze im *past progressive* mit den folgenden Angaben.

Yesterday at 11 am …

most people / not lie in their beds anymore ______________________________

my parents / not have breakfast anymore ______________________________

most people / not sleep anymore ______________________________

I / not lie in my bed anymore either ______________________________

I / not sit at the breakfast table anymore ______________________________

I not play / football ______________________________

I / sit on a chair ______________________________

I / do an English test* ______________________________

* to do a test (AmE: to take a test) = einen Test schreiben

214 When the doorbell rang yesterday at seven o'clock … I was just getting up.; my parents were having breakfast.; my father was reading the morning paper.; my sister was still sleeping.; our neighbors were still lying in their beds.; my younger brother was still dreaming.; other people were having a good time.

215 Yesterday at 11 am … most people were not lying in their beds anymore.; my parents were not having breakfast anymore.; most people were not sleeping anymore.; I was not lying in my bed anymore either.; I was not sitting at the breakfast table anymore.; I was not playing football.; I was sitting on a chair.; I was doing an English test.

216 ★★☆ Und was hast du gerade um 11 Uhr getan?

Vervollständige die Fragen und gib Kurzantworten. Pass beim Partizip Präsens auf die richtige Schreibung auf.

________ you (do) ______________ a test? No, ______________

________ your teachers (ask) ______________ questions? Yes, ______________

________ you (talk) ______________ to your neighbour? No, ______________

________ your neighbour (make) ______________ fun of you? Yes, ______________

________ you (cry) ______________? No, ______________

217 ★★☆ Neugierig bin ich nicht, aber …

Stelle die entsprechenden Fragen.

I called you yesterday evening and couldn't reach you …

What / you / do when I called? You / watch a film? What film / you / watch?

What / your parents / do? You talk / someone / on the phone? You have / dinner / with your family? What / you eat?

____

____

____

____

____

____

____

____

____

216 Were you doing a test? No, I wasn't.; Were your teachers asking questions? Yes, they were.; Were you talking to your neighbour? No, I wasn't.; Was your neighbour making fun of you? Yes, he was.; Were you crying? No, I wasn't.

217 What were you doing when I called? Were you watching a film? What film were you watching? What were your parents doing? Were you talking to someone on the phone? Were you having dinner with your family? What were you eating?

218 ★★☆ Das *simple past* der Vollverben

Bilde das *simple past* der folgenden Verben.

a) happen, knock, pass, push; ______________________

turn, watch, cheer, cook, talk; ______________________

answer, ask, climb, finish; ______________________

explain, guess, help, look; ______________________

stay, play, enjoy ______________________

b) love, dance, explore, agree ______________________

c) invite, hate, point, end, fold ______________________

d) hurry, cry, carry, tidy ______________________

e) plan, drop, stop, clap ______________________

219 ★★☆ Was weißt du noch?

Ergänze den Text.

1. Bei Verben, die das *simple past* regelmäßig bilden, wird ein __________ an den Infinitiv angehängt.
   Wo bereits ein *-e* vorhanden ist, entfällt dieses (z. B.: *dance* + *ed* = *danced*).
2. Die Endung *-ed* wird bei Verben, die auf ein gesprochenes / t / oder / d / enden, wie __________ ausgesprochen (z. B. *hate* + *ed* = *hated*).
3. Ein *-y* wird nach ______________ zu *ie*; nach ______________ bleibt es erhalten (z. B. *try* → *tried*, aber *play* → *played*).
4. Der letzte Konsonant bei einsilbigen Verben mit kurzem betonten Vokal wird __________ (z. B. *drop* → *dropped*).

218 a) happened, knocked, passed, pushed; turned, watched, cheered, cooked, talked; answered, asked, climbed, finished; explained, guessed, helped, looked; stayed, played, enjoyed; **b)** loved, danced, explored, agreed; **c)** invited, hated, pointed, ended, folded; **d)** hurried, cried, carried, tidied; **e)** planned, dropped, stopped, clapped
219 1. … wird ein *-ed* angehängt. **2.** … wie /id/ ausgesprochen. **3.** … nach Konsonant zu *ie*, nach Vokal bleibt es erhalten. **4.** … wird verdoppelt.

220 ★★☆ Unregelmäßige Formen

Bilde das *simple past* der folgenden Verben.

choose ______	eat ______	speak ______
come ______	fly ______	stand ______
do ______	fall ______	take ______
drive ______	feel ______	tell ______
keep ______	leave ______	throw ______
lose ______	make ______	know ______
meet ______	read ______	write ______
have ______	go ______	wear ______
hear ______	give ______	fight ______
hurt ______	hide ______	mean ______
sell ______	ride ______	find ______

221 ★★☆ Welches Verb passt nicht?

Bilde das *simple past* der folgenden Verben. Ein Verb passt jedoch nicht in die jeweilige Reihe. Unterstreiche es!

1. cut ______	get ______	put ______	cost ______
2. know ______	fly ______	grow ______	show ______
3. drink ______	sing ______	begin ______	win ______
4. sleep ______	keep ______	feel ______	see ______
5. catch ______	think ______	bring ______	buy ______

220 chose, came, did, drove, kept, lost, met, had, heard, hurt, sold; ate, flew, fell, felt, left, made, read, went, gave, hid, rode; spoke, stood, took, told, threw, knew, wrote, wore, fought, meant, found
221 1. cut, got, put, cost; **2.** knew, flew, grew, showed; **3.** drank, sang, began, won; **4.** slept, kept, felt, saw; **5.** caught, thought, brought, bought

222 ★★☆ Ein Einbruch

Gebrauche das *simple past*.

Yesterday the Masons / come home late. ______________________

They / open the door. ______________________

They / switch on the light. ______________________

They / go into the living-room. ______________________

Something / be / wrong. ______________________

They / notice it immediately. ______________________

The cupboards / be / all open. ______________________

They / see / all their things on the floor. ______________________

They immediately / understand. ______________________

Mr Mason / call the police. ______________________

223 ★★☆ Die Polizei ist da

Setze die Verben in das *simple past*.

Half an hour later the police ______________________. (arrive)

They ______________ in front of the Masons' house. (park)

They ______________ out of the car. (get)

The Masons ______________ the door. (open)

Three policemen ______________ the house. (enter)

They ______________ hello to the Masons. (say)

They ______________ them a lot of questions. (ask)

Then they ______________ a lot of pictures. (take)*

* ein Foto machen = to take a picture (NICHT to make!)

222 came, opened, switched, went, was, noticed, were, saw, understood, call

223 arrived, parked, got, opened, entered, said, asked, took

224 ★★☆ Ein schlauer Bursche

Setze die verneinten Vergangenheitsformen ein.

The police examined the rooms,

but they ______________ anything. (not find)

There ______________ any finger prints. (not be)

They ______________ any tools. (not see)

There ______________ any shoe prints on the floor. (not be)

The burglar ______________ an amateur. (not be)

He ______________ many mistakes. (not make)

He ______________ the police to catch him. (not want)

The police ______________ happy. (not be)

225 ★★☆ Weißt du noch ...?

Wie bildest du die Verneinung im *simple past*? Fülle die Lücken aus.

a) Du bildest die Verneinung mit ______________ oder __________ (Kurzform).

b) Danach folgt immer der ______________.

c) Bei *to be* steht keine Form von *to* ______________. Hier genügt ein __________.

d) Verneine die folgenden Sätze.

they saw ______________	they noticed ______________
they found ______________	they heard ______________
they listened ______________	this meant ______________
I understood ______________	they were ______________
I did ______________	we did ______________

224 they didn't find …; There weren't …; They didn't see …; There weren't …; The burglar was not …; He didn't make …; He didn't want …; The police were not…

225 a) *did not* oder *didn't*, **b)** Infinitiv, **c)** von *to do*. Hier genügt ein *not*. **d)** they didn't see, they didn't find, they didn't listen, I didn't understand, I didn't do; they didn't notice, they didn't hear, this didn't mean, they were not, we didn't do

226 ★★☆ Kein Verhör, aber Fragen

Stelle die Fragen der Polizisten.

a) You call us half an hour ago? ______________________________?

b) You leave the window open? ______________________________?

c) Anybody know that you were out tonight? ______________________________?

d) You turn the lights on? ______________________________?

e) You notice anything out of the ordinary*? ______________________________?

f) Your neighbour notice** anything? ______________________________?

g) You be out all evening? ______________________________?

h) You shut that door? ______________________________?

i) The burglar*** steal anything? ______________________________?

j) He open that safe? ______________________________?

* anything out of the ordinary = irgendwas Außergewöhnliches
** to notice = erkennen, mitbekommen
*** burglar = Einbrecher, Dieb

227 ★★☆ Was die Masons antworteten

Schaue dir die Fragen in Kurztest 226 noch einmal an. Gib dann die entsprechenden Kurzantworten.

a) Yes, ____________________

b) No, ____________________

c) No, nobody ____________________

d) Yes, ____________________

e) Yes, ____________________

f) No, ____________________

g) Yes, ____________________

h) No, ____________________

i) Yes, ____________________

j) Yes, ____________________

226 a) Did you call us …? **b)** Did you leave the window open? **c)** Did anybody know …? **d)** Did you turn the lights on? **e)** Did you notice anything …? **f)** Did your neighbour notice anything? **g)** Were you out all evening? **h)** Did you shut that door? **i)** Did the burglar steal anything? **j)** Did he open that safe?

227 a) Yes, we did. **b)** No, we didn't. **c)** No, nobody did. **d)** Yes, we did. **e)** Yes, we did. **f)** No, he / she didn't. **g)** Yes, we were. **h)** No, we didn't. **i)** Yes, he did. **j)** Yes, he did.

228 ★★☆ Wie die Geschichte weitergeht

Fülle den Text aus.

Though* the burglar ____________ a beginner (not be), the police ____________ him and ____________ him (catch / arrest**). The next day they ____________ him to a particular room (take), ____________ him to sit down (tell) and ____________ to ask him a lot of questions (begin).

* though = obwohl
** to arrest = festnehmen

229 ★★☆ Ein Verhör

Stelle die entsprechenden Fragen.

They asked him:

- how get into the house
- what find in the house
- how open the safe
- what in the safe
- what take out of the safe
- how long stay in the house
- when leave the house

?

____

____

____

____

____

____

____

228 Though the burglar was not a beginner, they caught him and arrested him. The next day they took him to a particular room, told him to sit down and began to ask him a lot of questions.
229 How did you get into the house? What did you find in the house? How did you open the safe? What was in the safe? What did you take out of the safe? How long did you stay in the house? When did you leave the house?

230 ★★☆ Was weißt du noch?

Beantworte die folgenden Fragen.

1. Mit welchen Fragewörtern fragst du nach dem Subjekt und dem Objekt?

   ● who ● why ● what ● how

2. Bei welchen Fragen darfst du *to do* nicht gebrauchen? ______________________

   ____

3. Und wie ist es bei Fragen nach anderen Satzteilen? Was musst du dann gebrauchen?

   ____

   ____

231 ★★☆ Weitere Fragen

Stelle Fragen nach den markierten Substantiven.

The burglar broke into the house.

____

The neighbours didn't see **him.**

____

The burglar opened **the safe.**

____

The burglar took the money out of the safe.

____

The burglar took **the money** out of the safe.

____

230 1. who / what, **2.** Bei nicht verneinten Fragen nach dem Subjekt. **3.** Bei Fragen nach allen anderen Satzteilen muss man *to do* gebrauchen.
231 Who broke into the house? Who didn't the neighbours see? What did he open? Who took the money out of the safe? What did he take out of the safe?

232 ★★☆ Eine Pressekonferenz

Stelle die Fragen der Reporter an die Polizei.

How be able / to find the burglar?

______________________________ ?

What mistakes / he make?

______________________________ ?

Anybody / help him?

______________________________ ?

When / break into the house?

______________________________ ?

What / he steal?

______________________________ ?

233 ★★☆ Und was fragte man ihn im Gefängnis?

Stelle die entsprechenden Fragen.

Why / you / break into that house? ______________________________ ?

Who / tell you to break into that house? ______________________________ ?

You / alone when you broke into the house? ______________________________ ?

What / you hope to find there? ______________________________ ?

You / spend all the money you stole? ______________________________ ?

You / give the money back? ______________________________ ?

What / you need the money for? ______________________________ ?

232 How were you able to find the burglar? What mistake did he make? Did anybody help him? When did he break into the house? What did he steal?

233 Why did you break into that house? Who told you to break into that house? Were you alone when you broke into the house? What did you hope to find there? Did you spend all the money you stole? Did you give the money back? What did you need the money for?

234 ★★☆ Im Schwimmbad

Bilde das *past progressive* mit den folgenden Angaben (Achtung: Einmal geht es nicht!).

Yesterday Tom and some others went to the swimming pool. When they arrived …

the sun / shine ______

the sun / not hide behind clouds ______

many people / be / there ______

many people / swim in the pool ______

others / talk to their friends ______

others / play football ______

some people / sleep ______

some / read a book or a magazine ______

some / lie in the sun and dream ______

235 ★★☆ Ein ruhiger Nachmittag

Setze die Formen des *past progressive* ein.

Everything was peaceful.

People not shout ______

People not run around ______

People not fight ______

Mike lie peacefully in the grass ______

Ken not scream at the others ______

Only John tell silly stories ______

234 … the sun was shining.; … the sun was not hiding behind clouds.; … many people were there.; … many people were swimming in the pool.; … others were talking to their friends.; … others were playing football.; … some people were sleeping.; … some were reading a book or a magazine.; … some were lying in the sun and dreaming.

235 People were not shouting. People were not running around. People were not fighting. Mike was lying peacefully in the grass.; Ken was not screaming at the others. Only John was telling silly stories.

236 ★★☆ Fragen an Tom

Ergänze die Fragen und gib Kurzantworten.

What ______________ you doing at 5 o'clock yesterday afternoon?

a) __________ you having a swim? No, ______________________

b) __________ you still lying in the grass? No, ______________________

c) __________ you packing your things? Yes, ______________________

d) __________ Ken packing his things, too? Yes, ______________________

e) __________ Mike still listening to music? No, ______________________

f) __________ John still talking of Alice? Yes, ______________________

g) __________ the others listening? No, ______________________

237 ★★☆ Zur selben Zeit …

Setze die entsprechenden Formen des *past progressive* ein.

While Tom ______________ his things (pack), other people ______________ their things, too (pack). Others ______________ still ______________ (swim). They ______________ their friends (call) or ______________ in the grass (lie). The sun ______________ still ______________ (shine). The sky was a bit cloudy, but it ______________ (be / not rain).

While Tom ______________ home (go), his mother ______________ tea (make) and ______________ the table (set). The water ______________ nearly ______________ (boil) when Tom finally got home.

236 What were you doing at 5 o'clock yesterday afternoon? **a)** Were …/No, I wasn't. **b)** Were …/No, I wasn't. **c)** Were …/Yes, I was. **d)** Was …/Yes, he was. **e)** Was …/No, he wasn't. **f)** Was …/Yes, he was. **g)** Were …/No, they weren't.

237 While Tom was packing his things, other people were packing their things, too. Others were still swimming. They were calling their friends or lying in the grass. The sun was still shining. The sky was a bit cloudy, but it wasn't raining. While Tom was going home, his mother was making tea and setting the table. The water was nearly boiling …

238 ★★☆ Ein Ausflug Teil I

Gestern besuchte Toms Klasse den Zoo von Bristol. Hier ist Toms Bericht. Setze die Verben in das *simple past*.

Yesterday we ______________ to the zoo with Mr Winterbottom, our biology teacher (go). We ______________ to the bus stop (walk). We ______________ on the bus (get). In the bus we ______________ for our seats (look). Everybody ______________ happy (be). But soon the trouble ______________ (start). Mike ______________ (not feel) very well. He ______________ sick (get). It ______________ terrible (be)!

239 ★★☆ Ein Ausflug Teil II

Hier ist einiges durcheinandergeraten. Bringe die Sätze in die richtige Reihenfolge und setze die Verben in das *simple past*.

- The bus ______________ at the zoo. (arrive)
- He ______________ angry. (become)
- Some pupils ______________ to run around inside the bus. (start)
- Others ______________ to eat their crisps. (begin)
- The bus driver ______________ this. (see)
- He ______________ to shout. (begin)
- There ______________ crisps everywhere. (be)
- We ______________ off the bus. (get)
- I ______________ happy. (be)
- We ______________ there. (be)
- Other pupils ______________ their feet on the seats. (put)

238 Yesterday we went to the zoo … We walked to the bus stop. We got on the bus. In the bus we looked for our seats. Everybody was happy. But soon the trouble started. Mike didn't feel very well. He got sick. It was terrible!

239 Some pupils started to run around in the bus. Others began to eat their crisps. There were crisps everywhere. Other pupils put their feet on the seats. The bus driver saw this. He became angry. He began to shout. The bus arrived at the zoo. We got off the bus. I was happy. We were there.

240 ★★☆ Toms Bericht

Verbinde die Sätze in den Kurztests Nr. 238 und 239 mit den folgenden Signalwörtern: ***first, then, the next moment, later, when, soon, finally, suddenly.***

____

____

____

____

____

____

241 ★★☆ Verhalten im Zoo

Bevor sie den Zoo betraten, erzählte ihnen Mr. Winterbottom, was er bei seinem letzten Zoobesuch gesehen hatte. Setze die Verben in die Vergangenheit und füge die entsprechenden Signalwörter ein.

There were people who …

a) ______________________ to feed the animals. (always try)

b) Others ______________________ to make the animals angry. (sometimes try)

c) They ______________________ on their cages. (sometimes knock)

d) Or they ______________________ loud noises. (often make)

e) They ______________________ things at them. (often throw)

f) They ______________________ fun of them. (usually make)

g) They ______________________ nice to them. (be seldom)

240 Yesterday we went to the zoo. First we walked to the bus stop. Then we got on the bus. In the bus we looked for our seats. Everybody was happy. But soon the trouble started. Mike suddenly didn't feel very well. The next moment he got sick. Suddenly some pupils started to run around inside the bus. Others began to eat their crisps. Soon there were crisps everywhere. Other pupils put their feet on the seats. When the bus driver saw this, he became angry. He began to shout. At last, the bus arrived at the zoo. When we got off the bus, I was happy that we were finally there.

241 a) always tried **b)** sometimes tried **c)** sometimes knocked **d)** often made **e)** often threw things **f)** usually made **g)** were seldom

242 ★★☆ Jungtiere im Zoo

Setze die Präpositionen ein und schreibe auf, wann die Jungtiere geboren wurden.

two young wolves	elephants	
_____ February	Dora _____ 2007	Dina _____ 2006

zebra	polar bear	gorilla
_____ 4th March	_____ Wednesday, 23rd May	_____ Tuesday last week

Beginne wie folgt:

The two young wolves ____

____

____

____

243 ★★☆ Was weißt du noch?

Schaue dir die Kurztests 238 bis 242 noch einmal an. Sie sagen dir, wann du das *simple past* im Englischen benutzen musst.

1. In den Kurztests 238 und 239 berichtet oder erzählt jemand etwas, das:

   ● bereits vorbei ist. ● noch andauert. ● bis in die Zukunft noch andauert.

2. Ein solcher Bericht oder eine solche Erzählung besteht aus Handlungen oder Vorgängen, die aufeinanderfolgen. Solche Handlungen oder Vorgänge stehen im Englischen im:

   ______________________.

3. Im Kurztest 241 wird das *simple past* für wiederholte und gewohnheitsmäßige Handlungen benutzt. Im Kurztest 242 steht das *simple past* für Handlungen oder Vorgänge, die ______________ sind. (Signalwörter: *yesterday*, *last*, *ago*, *in* + Datum …)

242 The two young wolves were born in February. The elephants were born in 2007 and in 2006. The zebra was born on 4th March. The polar bear was born on Wednesday, 23rd May. The gorilla was born on Tuesday last week.
243 1. bereits vorbei ist; **2.** simple past; **3.** vorüber.

244 ★★☆ Im Affenhaus

Setze die richtigen Verbformen ein.

All the children ____________ to see the young polar bear, but Mr	want
Winterbottom ____________ them that the bear ____________	tell / be
still too young to leave its cage. So they ____________ over to see	go
the monkeys. When they ____________ there, feeding-time ________	get / be
over. But some of the monkeys ____________ still very hungry. They	be
____________ their bananas or __________ on their carrots and	eat / nibble*
apples. Others ____________ so hungry anymore. Some ________	not be
______________ in a corner. Others ______________ some-	sit / hide
where in their cage and some __________________. Two gorillas	sleep
______________ each other. A young one ______________	chase / stand
near the window of his cage and ______________ at the visitors.	look

*to nibble = (an)knabbern

245 ★★☆ Das *simple past* und das *past progressive*

Finde Beispiele für die folgenden Erklärungen in dem obigen Text.

1. Hast du das System kapiert? Du gebrauchst das *simple past* für Handlungen, die neu einsetzen, sich wiederholen oder – wie in einer Geschichte – aufeinander folgen.

   ____

2. Das *past progressive* gebrauchst du dagegen für Handlungen, die zu einem bestimmten Zeitpunkt der Vergangenheit noch nicht vorüber sind, sondern gerade ablaufen.

   ____

244 All the children wanted to see the young polar bear, but Mr Winterbottom told them that the bear was still too young to leave its cage. So they went over to see the monkeys. When they got there, feeding-time was over. But some of the monkeys were still very hungry. They were eating their bananas or nibbling on their carrots and apples. Others were not so hungry anymore. Some were sitting in a corner. Others were hiding somewhere in their cage, and some were sleeping. Two gorillas were chasing each other. A young one was standing near the window of his cage and looking at the visitors.

245 1. So they went over to the monkeys' house. When they got there … **2.** They were eating their bananas, nibbling on their carrots, etc. Alles geschieht in dem Augenblick, wo die Kinder sie sehen.

246 ★★☆ Mike und das Gorillababy

Setze die richtigen Verbformen ein.

But where ________________ the baby gorilla (be)? ____________ he in the cage or somewhere else (be)? Then, suddenly, Mike ________________ (see) him. The baby ________________ (lie) beside its mother and ________________ to get some milk (try). "Isn't he cute?", a girl ______________ (shout). "Look at him! He ____________ just ________________ there like my baby brother (lie)." Everybody ________________ when she ________________ that (laugh / say).

247 ★★★ Die Heimfahrt

Setze das *simple past* oder das *past progressive* ein.

It _________ six o'clock (be), and the zoo _______________ its doors (close). "Come on," Mr Winterbottom ____________ (shout), "the bus is waiting for us." And indeed it _______ (be). It ________________ there (wait). Their bus driver ________ there, too (be). He ________________ angry anymore (not be), but before they _______________ on the bus (get), he __________ (say) that he wanted to tell them a few things …

So they all __________ in (get) and ____________ down in their seats (sit). Or at least most of them ____________ (do). Mr Winterbottom _____________ (tell) them again and again not to run around, but some of them ________________ (not listen).

And so it _________________________ (happen).

246 But where was the baby gorilla? Was he in the cage or somewhere else? Then, suddenly, Mike saw him. The baby was lying beside its mother and was trying to get some milk. "Isn't he cute?", a girl shouted. "Look at him! He is just lying there like my baby brother." Everybody laughed when she said that.

247 It was six o'clock and the zoo was closing its doors. "Come on," Mr Winterbottom shouted, … And indeed it was. It was waiting there. Their bus driver was there, too. He wasn't angry anymore, but before they got on the bus, he said that he wanted to tell them … So they all got in and sat down in their seats. Or at least most of them did. Mr Winterbottom told them again and again not to run around, but some of them didn't listen. And so it happened.

248 ★★★ Ein Unfall

Füge die richtigen Verbformen ein.

Suddenly the bus ________________ to a stop (come). John ________________ still ________________ (stand), and he ________________ (fall) onto the floor and ________________ (hit) his head on a seat. One of the pupils ________________ Mr Winterbottom at once (call). He ________________ very angry (become) when he ________________ (see) that John ________________ (lie) on the floor. "Why don't you listen?" he ________________ (shout). But when he ________________ (see) that John's mouth ________________ (bleed), he ________________ (run) to the bus driver and ________________ (ask) him to call a doctor. A few minutes later an ambulance ________________ (arrive). Two paramedics* ________________ (come) into the bus. They ________________ (have) a look at the boy. Then they ________________ (fetch) a stretcher. They ________________ (put) John on it and ________________ (load**) him onto the ambulance.

* paramedic (ambulance man) = Sanitäter, Rettungsassistent, Notarzt
** to load = befördern

249 ★★★ In der Notaufnahme I

Es waren viele Leute in der Notaufnahme. Einige unterhielten sich und erzählten, weshalb sie hier waren. Setze die richtigen Verbformen der folgenden Verben ein.

I ________________ a shower when I ________________. (have / slip)

I ________________ the windows when one window ________________, and the broken glass ________________ my hands. (clean / break / cut)

And what did John tell them? ________________________________

____

248 Suddenly the bus came to a stop. John was still standing when it stopped, and he fell onto the floor and hit his head on a seat. One of the pupils called Mr Winterbottom at once. He became very angry when he saw that John was lying on the floor. „Why don't you listen?" he shouted. But when he saw that John's mouth was bleeding, he ran to the bus driver and asked him to call a doctor. A few minutes later an ambulance arrived. Two paramedics came into the bus. They had a look at the boy. Then they fetched a stretcher. They put John on it and loaded him onto the ambulance.

249 I was having a shower when I slipped. I crashed onto the floor. I was cleaning the windows when one window broke, and the broken glass cut my hands. John: I was running around on the bus when it suddenly stopped. I fell and hit my head on a seat.

250 ★★★ In der Notaufnahme II

Unterstreiche im Text die Hilfsverben. Setze dann den ganzen Text in das *simple past*.

The paramedics take John to the accident and emergency department*. He must wait for a doctor. He feels better, but he can't move. So he can only stay where he is. He can't walk around the room. When the nurse comes in, she tells him that he must stay where he is and that he mustn't stand up. But she also tells him that he needn't worry.

____

____

____

____

* Notaufnahme = accident and emergency department, A&E (AmE = emergency room, ER)

251 ★★★ Wie lauten ihre Vergangenheitsformen?

Ergänze die Vergangenheitsform. Sieh dir dann die Lösungen an und korrigiere, was du eventuell falsch gemacht hast.

can	____________	(konnte)
can't	____________	(konnte nicht)
can / may	____________	(durfte)
can't / may not	____________	(durfte nicht)
mustn't	____________	(durfte nicht)
needn't	____________	(musste nicht, brauchte nicht)

Lerne dann diese Vergangenheitsformen auswendig!

250 must, can't, can, can't, must, mustn't, needn't; The paramedics took John to the accident and emergency department. He had to wait for a doctor. He felt better, but he couldn't move. So he could only stay where he was. He couldn't walk around the room. When the nurse came in, she told him that he had to stay where he was and that he was not allowed to stand up. But she also told him that he didn't have to worry.

251 konnte = could; konnte nicht = couldn't; durfte = was / were allowed to; durfte nicht = was / were not allowed to; mustn't = was not / were not allowed to; musste nicht, brauchte nicht = didn't have to / didn't need to

252 ★★☆ Was dann geschah

Setze die entsprechenden Vergangenheitsformen ein! Pass dabei auf, ob diesen Formen ein *to* folgt!

John ______________________ go home. (durfte)

He ______________________ stay in hospital. (musste nicht)

He ______________________ go to school. (brauchte nicht)

He ______________________ stay in bed for three days. (musste)

His friends ______________________ come to see him, … (konnten)

but they ______________________ stay more than half an hour. (durften nicht)

After 30 minutes, they ______________________ to leave. (mussten)

253 ★★☆ Besorgte Fragen

Stelle John die folgenden Fragen.

you / go home? ______________________ (durftest)

you / stay in hospital? ______________________ (musstest nicht)

you / go to school? ______________________ (brauchtest nicht)

you / stay in bed? ______________________ (musstest)

you / watch TV? ______________________ (durftest)

your friends / visit you? ______________________ (durften)

they / stay with you? ______________________ (durften)

they / talk with you? ______________________ (konnten)

When they / leave? ______________________ (mussten)

252 John was allowed to go home. He didn't have to stay in hospital. He didn't have to go to school. He had to stay in bed for three days. His friends could come to see him, but they were not allowed to stay more than half an hour. After 30 minutes they had to leave.

253 Were you allowed to go home? Didn't you have to stay in hospital? Didn't you have to go to school? Did you have to stay in bed? Were you allowed to watch TV? Were your friends allowed to visit you? Were they allowed to stay with you? Could they talk with you? When did they have to leave?

254 ★★☆ John ist wieder zurück

Gib Kurzantworten auf die Fragen, die seine Klassenkameraden ihm stellen.

Did you have to stay in hospital? No, ____________________

Did you have to stay in bed? Yes, ____________________

Did you have to take any medicine? Yes, ____________________

Were you allowed to watch TV? Yes, ____________________

Did you have to do any homework? No, ____________________

Were you allowed to call your friends? Yes, ____________________

Could you talk to them on the phone? Yes, ____________________

Were your friends allowed to visit you? Yes, ____________________

255 ★★★ Und nun zu dir und deinen Freunden …

Stelle einem Freund von dir die Fragen. Gebrauche die Hilfsverben.

The last time you were ill …

____________________ go to hospital? (Musstest du)

____________________ stay in bed? (Wie lange musstest du)

____________________ see you? (Wie oft musste der Arzt)

____________________ get out of bed on your own*? (Konntest du)

____________________ do in hospital? (Was durftest du nicht)

____________________ do any homework? (Musstest du)

__________ your friends __________ visit you? (Wie oft durften)

____________________ to go home? (Wann durftest)

* on your own = alleine, ohne Hilfe von anderen

254 No, I didn't.; Yes, I did.; Yes, I did.; Yes, I was.; No, I didn't.; Yes, I was.; Yes, I could.; Yes, they were.
255 Did you have to go to hospital? How long did you have to stay in bed? How often did the doctor have to see you? Could you get out of bed on your own? What weren't you allowed to do in hospital? Did you have to do any homework? How often were your friends allowed to visit you? When were you allowed to go home?

256 ★★☆ Ein Quiz

Kreuze die richtige Antwort an.

1. Nach *can, may, must, needn't, mustn't* steht in der Gegenwart immer ein Infinitiv.

   ○ ja ○ nein

2. Vor diesem Infinitiv steht nie ein *to*.

   ○ ja ○ nein

3. Diese Hilfsverben haben bis auf *can / can't* keine eigene Vergangenheitsform.

   ○ ja ○ nein

4. Für *must / needn't* musst du in der Vergangenheit die entsprechenden Formen von *to have* to gebrauchen.

   ○ ja ○ nein

5. *to have to* ist ein Vollverb. Es wird im Unterschied zu *to be allowed to* mit *to do* gebraucht.

   ○ ja ○ nein

257 ★★☆ Drakonische Maßnahmen

Setze die entsprechenden Hilfsverben ein.

The next time Mr Winterbottom went to the zoo on a class trip …

All of the pupils ____________________ sit in their seats.

Nobody ____________________ to stand up.

Nobody ____________________ to run around in the bus.

If anybody did, he or she ____________________ do a lot of homework.

They ____________________ walk home.

They ____________________ to go to zoo with him again.

256 **1.** ja; **2.** ja; **3.** ja; **4.** ja; **5.** ja
257 All of the pupils had to sit in their seats.; Nobody was allowed to stand up.; Nobody was allowed to run around on the bus.; If anybody did, he or she had to do a lot of homework.; They had to walk home.; They were not allowed to go to the zoo with him again.

258 ★★☆ Ein armer Mann

Gebrauche das Vollverb *to have* für *have got*.

Mr Fletcher hasn't got anything. ______________________

He hasn't got a house. ______________________

He hasn't got a wife. ______________________

He hasn't got a family. ______________________

He hasn't got a job. ______________________

He hasn't got any money. ______________________

He hasn't got a car. ______________________

He hasn't got any friends. ______________________

He hasn't got anything. ______________________

259 ★★☆ Einmal anders gefragt …

Stelle dieselben Fragen mit *to have*.

Have your parents got a house? ______________________

Has Debbie got a hamster? ______________________

Have her parents got a cat? ______________________

Have you got a problem? ______________________

Has Mike got a bike? ______________________

Have these people got the tickets? ______________________

Has this girl got a friend? ______________________

Have you got a lot of courage? ______________________

258 Mr Fletcher doesn't have anything. He doesn't have a house. He doesn't have a wife. He doesn't have a family. He doesn't have a job. He doesn't have any money. He doesn't have a car. He doesn't have any friends. He doesn't have anything.

259 Do your parents have a house? Does Debbie have a hamster? Do her parents have a cat? Do you have a problem? Does Mike have a bike? Do these people have the tickets? Does this girl have a friend? Do you have a lot of courage?

260 ★★☆ Kurzantworten

Gib Kurzantworten. Achte dabei auf die Fragen.

a) Have you got a big family? No, ______
b) Have you got any pets? Yes, ______
c) Has your sister got a baby? No, ______
d) Does your grandma have a motorbike? Yes, ______
e) Do you have problems with your teachers? No, ______
f) Do you have problems at school? No, ______
g) Do your parents have problems with you? No, ______
h) Has Debbie got any letters from you? No, ______
i) Do you have a message for me? Yes, ______
j) Have you got any time for me? No, ______
k) Don't you have a little money for me? No, ______
l) Haven't you got anything else for me? No, ______

261 ★★☆ Wo liegt der Unterschied?

Schaue dir die folgenden Sätze genau an. Ergänze dann den Text.

She **has got** a house. She's **having** a cup of tea.

She **has** a house. She **has** a bath every evening.

1. *have got* und *to have* bedeuten „haben" im Sinne von ______.
2. *to have* kann ganz andere Bedeutungen haben, wie in der folgenden Wendung:

   to have a bath = ______. Hier ist *have got* nicht möglich.

260 a) No, I/we haven't. **b)** Yes, I/we have. **c)** No, she hasn't. **d)** Yes, she does. **e)** No, I/we don't. **f)** No, I/we don't. **g)** No, they don't. **h)** No, she hasn't. **i)** Yes, I/we do. **j)** No, I/we haven't. **k)** No, I/we don't. **l)** No, I/we haven't.
261 1. *have got* und *to have* bedeuten *haben* im Sinne von *besitzen*. **2.** *to have a bath* = ein Bad nehmen

262 ★★☆ Ausdrücke mit *to have*

Ordne die Ausdrücke mit *to have* den deutschen Bedeutungen zu.

to have an accident	ein Kind haben, ein Kind bekommen
to have fun	einen Tag frei haben
to have a bath	Spaß haben, sich amüsieren
to have breakfast	Mittag essen
to have a day off	plaudern, Schwätzen halten
to have lunch	eine Pause machen
to have a chat	einen Unfall haben
to have a break	ein Bad nehmen, baden
to have a baby	frühstücken
to have a shower	duschen
to have an argument	(sich) streiten

263 ★★☆ Hast du sie gelernt?

Dann setze die entsprechenden Wendungen sinngemäß ein.

a) It's twelve o'clock. Let's ______________________.

b) Oh dear, you smell bad! Go to the bathroom and ______________________.

c) My aunt is pregnant*. She will ______________________ a baby soon.

d) Be careful when you ride your bike! Don't ______________________.

e) You're going skiing this weekend? ______________________! Break a leg!

* pregnant = schwanger

262 to have an accident = einen Unfall haben; to have fun = Spaß haben, sich amüsieren; to have a bath = ein Bad nehmen, sich baden; to have breakfast = frühstücken; to have a day off = einen freien Tag haben; to have lunch = Mittag essen; to have a chat = plaudern, Schwätzchen halten; to have a break = eine Pause machen; to have a baby = ein Kind haben, ein Kind bekommen; to have a shower = sich duschen; to have an argument = streiten

263 a) Let's have lunch. **b)** … and have a bath / shower. **c)** … have a baby soon. **d)** … Don't have an accident. **e)** Have fun!

264 ★★☆ Badezimmerprobleme

Have got **oder** ***have*****? Wo kannst du** ***have got*** **nicht einsetzen?**

It's early in the morning. The children are getting up for school. They always ________ an argument before they decide who can go to the bathroom first. The reason is that Alice always needs such a long time in the bathroom. First she ________ a shower, and then she washes her hair. After that she ________ a chat with her dolls. She keeps her dolls in the bathroom, and Alice ________ many of them. So when Alice goes to the bathroom first, the others ________ very little time to use it. They can't ________ a shower or a bath. They can only wash their faces, brush their teeth and then – maybe – they have time to ________ a very quick breakfast. Then they rush off to school on their bikes.

265 ★★☆ Ein genauerer Blick …

Welche Formen von ***have/have got*** **musst du einsetzen?**

Alice, can we come in now? No, you can't, I ________ a shower.

Come on, Alice, hurry up! We want to ________ a shower, too.

Just go and ________ your breakfast. You can ________ a shower after that.

Five minutes later they come back, but Alice is still in the bathroom. She ________ a chat with her dolls now. They ________ the day off, so they ________ a lot of time. So there is no need to ________ an argument today!

264 They always have an argument … First she has a shower … After that she has a chat with her dolls. … Alice has / has got many of them. So when Alice goes to the bathroom first, the others have / have got little time to use it. They can't have a shower or a bath. … they have time to have a very quick breakfast …

265 … No, you can't, I am having a shower. Come on, Alice, hurry up! We want to have a shower, too. Just go and have your breakfast. You can have a shower after that. … She is having a chat with her dolls now. They have the day off, so they have / have got a lot of time. So there is no need to have an argument today!

266 ★★☆ Was du schon alles lernen musstest

Schreibe auf, was kleine Kinder alles lernen müssen und nicht müssen.

Young kids / babies have to learn / don't have to learn

to walk	to go to the toilet	to eat by themselves
to shoot a gun	to watch TV	to change their own pampers
to do the cooking	to earn money	to get dressed
to help others	to play poker	to fly an airplane

____

____

____

267 ★★☆ Und das Lernen geht weiter

Bilde Fragen und gib die entsprechenden Kurzantworten.

Beispiel: *Do you have to go to school? Yes, I do. No, I don't.*

a) ________ you ________ do your homework? ________

b) ________________ make fun of others? ________

c) ________________ find out what you like? ________

d) ________________ like everybody? ________

e) ________________ like all subjects? ________

f) ________________ be like everybody? ________

g) ________________ talk to everyone? ________

266 Young kids / babies have to learn: to walk, to go to the toilet, to eat by themselves, to get dressed, to help others. They don't have to learn: to shoot a gun, to watch TV, to change their own pampers, to do the cooking, to earn money, to play poker, to fly an airplane.
267 a) Do you have to do your homework? – Yes, I do. / No, I don't. **b)** Do you have to make fun of others? – Yes, I do. / No, I don't. **c)** Do you have to find out what you like? – Yes, I do. / No, I don't. **d)** Do you have to like everybody? – Yes, I do. / No, I don't. **e)** Do you have to like all subjects? – Yes, I do. / No, I don't. **f)** Do you have to be like everybody? – Yes, I do. / No, I don't. **g)** Do you have to talk to everyone? – Yes, I do. / No, I don't.

268 ★★☆ Auch deine Eltern müssen Dinge tun …

Bilde 4 Sätze mit den folgenden Angaben.

Beispiel: They had to clean their car though they didn't want to.

pay the bills ______________________________.

clean the flat ______________________________.

go to work ______________________________.

listen to me ______________________________.

269 ★★★ *Must* und *to have to*

a) Lies den Text durch und finde die richtige Bedeutung der zwei folgenden Sätze.

Müssen kann im Englischen mit *to have to* und mit *must* übersetzt werden. Allerdings werden beide Ausdrücke unterschiedlich verwendet. Das Verb *to have to* drückt ein Müssen aus, das von außen / von jemand anderem kommt. (Beispiel: **I have to work**. Denn, wenn ich nicht arbeite, verdiene ich kein Geld zum Leben.) Bei *must* ist das Müssen dagegen oft ein innerer Zwang. (Beispiel: **I really must go now**. Denn ich möchte meine Freunde nicht warten lassen.)

1. *I must see you.* — a) My mother told me to see you.

2. *I have to see you.* — b) I really love you and can't live without you.

Im *simple past* gibt es diesen Unterschied allerdings nicht mehr. Hier heißt es immer "I had to" = „Ich musste".

I ____________ see you.

b) Setze *must* oder *have* to ein.

1. I really ________________ go now. My parents are waiting for me.

2. Where is Debbie? I ________________ see her. I can't live without her.

3. I am afraid I can't come this afternoon. My mother told me I ________________ do my homework first.

4. I ________________ learn English. I need it for my job.

268 They had to (pay the bills / clean the flat / go to work / listen to me) though they didn't want to.
269 a) 1b), 2a); I had to see you.; **b) 1.** must, **2.** must, **3.** have to, **4.** have to

270 ★☆☆ Wünsche

Setze *to* ein, wo es fehlt.

a) What do you want to do in your life?

	______	become a pilot.
	______	see the world.
	______	a lot of money.
I want	______	spend it with you.
	______	five children.
	______	get a good job.

b) *to want* entspricht dem Deutschen ______________. Folgt ein Verb, dann musst du nach *to want* ein ________ einsetzen.

271 ★☆☆ Was möchtest du?

Setze *to* ein, wo es nötig ist.

	______	a cup of tea?
	______	some orange juice?
	______	have a drink?
Would you like	______	some more meat?
	______	go out with me?
	______	be my friend?

Wo liegt der Unterschied zwischen **would like (to)** und **to want (to)**?

____

270 a) I want to become a pilot. I want to see the world. I want a lot of money. I want to spend it with you. I want five children. I want to get a good job. **b)** to want = wollen; *to want to* + Verb

271 a) Would you like a cup of tea? Would you like some orange juice? Would you like to have a drink? Would you like some more meat? Would you like to go out with me? Would you like to be my friend?
b) *I'd like to … (I would like to)* ist höflicher als *I want to …*; *Would like to …* bedeutet „ich möchte", *want to …* bedeutet „ich will".

272 ★★☆ *Could*

Schaue dir die folgenden Sätze genau an und beantworte dann die Fragen.

Could you help me, please?

Could you come at three o'clock?

Could your sister come, too?

When we have finished, we could go for a walk.

Or we could have a drink somewhere.

a) Was bedeutet *could* in diesen Sätzen? Was kann *could* noch bedeuten?

____

b) Worum handelt es sich bei diesen Sätzen? Was drücken sie aus?

____

273 ★★☆ Tea time

Übersetze die folgenden Sätze.

Möchtest du noch etwas Zucker?

____

Könntest du mir ein Stück Kuchen geben?

____

Willst du noch etwas Milch?

____

Ich will nicht nach Hause gehen.

____

272 a) *Could* bedeutet hier „ könnte(st)“. *Could* kann auch noch „konnte“ bedeuten. **b)** Mit *could* (könnte) kannst du höflich fragen oder ein Angebot oder eine Möglichkeit ausdrücken.

273 Would you like some more sugar? Could you give me a piece of cake? Do you want some more milk? I don't want to go home.

274 ★☆☆ Wie kann ich helfen?

Mache Vorschläge mit *shall*.

buy a sandwich for you / do it for you / keep you company / carry it for you / find a place for you to sleep / explain it to you

"My schoolbag is so heavy." ______________________

"I'm so tired." ______________________

"I'm so hungry." ______________________

"I can't do my homework." ______________________

"This exercise is so difficult." ______________________

"I am so lonely." ______________________

275 ★☆☆ Was kann man tun?

Gib Ratschläge mit *should* (= sollte). Welche Sätze passen zusammen?

a) "I'm so tired."	not eat so much
b) "My tests are so bad."	study* harder
c) "TV is boring."	ask her out on a date
d) "My jeans don't fit anymore."	look for them
e) "I'm getting so fat."	not stay up so late
f) "My skirt is so dirty."	go home now
g) "My room is a real mess."	wash it
h) "I've lost my keys."	tidy it up
i) "Alice likes me."	not watch so much TV
j) "My parents are waiting for me."	buy new ones

* to study = studieren, lernen/pauken

274 Shall I carry it for you? Shall I find a place for you to sleep? Shall I buy a sandwich for you? Shall I do it for you? Shall I explain it to you? Shall I keep you company?
275 a) You shouldn't stay up so late. **b)** You should study harder. **c)** You shouldn't watch so much TV. **d)** You should buy new ones. **e)** You shouldn't eat so much. **f)** You should wash it. **g)** You should tidy it up. **h)** You should look for them. **i)** You should ask her out on a date. **j)** You should go home now.

276 ★★☆ Das *past participle* – regelmäßige Bildung

Wie du weißt, wird das *present perfect* mit den Formen von *have* und dem Partizip der Vergangenheit gebildet. Die Formen von *have* kennst du, aber weißt du auch noch, wie das Partizip gebildet wird? Bilde das *past participle* von den folgenden Verben:

talk ______________________ dance ______________________

end ______________________ play ______________________

try ______________________ return ______________________

carry ______________________ kill ______________________

drop ______________________ stop ______________________

look ______________________ die ______________________

tie ______________________ paint ______________________

Erinnern dich diese Formen an etwas? Richtig: Sie werden genauso gebildet wie die regelmäßigen Formen des ______________________ .

277 ★★☆ Unregelmäßige Partizipien

Wie lauten die *past participles* der folgenden Verben?

be ______________________ have ______________________

choose ______________________ lose ______________________

fly ______________________ know ______________________

feel ______________________ fall ______________________

write ______________________ think ______________________

go ______________________ do ______________________

say ______________________ tell ______________________

wear ______________________ buy ______________________

276 talked, ended, tried, carried, dropped, looked, tied; danced, played, returned, killed, stopped, died, painted …
Sie werden genauso gebildet wie die regelmäßigen Formen des *simple past*.
277 been, chosen, flown, felt, written, gone, said, worn; had, lost, known, fallen, thought, done, told, bought.

278 ★★☆ Und wie steht es mit dem Infinitiv?

Wie heißt der Infinitiv der folgenden Verbformen? Achte auf die Schreibung!

chosen ____	lost ____
bought ____	meant ____
written ____	fed ____
held ____	fled ____
worn ____	felt ____
drawn ____	met ____
woken ____	given ____
told ____	sold ____
left ____	flown ____
found ____	shaken ____
hidden ____	bled ____
shown ____	broken ____

279 ★★☆ Was passt nicht?

Unterstreiche die Verben, deren Partizip nicht in die jeweilige Reihe passt.

a) have	hurt	put	cut	sit	cost
b) teach	fight	think	drink	buy	bring
c) spend	sleep	build	hear	lose	keep
d) make	take	fall	write	forget	ride
e) drink	run	swim	think	ring	sink

278 choose, buy, write, hold, wear, draw, wake, tell, leave, find, hide, show; lose, mean, feed, flee, feel, meet, give, sell, fly, shake, bleed, break
279 a) have **b)** drink **c)** hear, **d)** make **e)** think

280 ★★☆ Ein bewegter Tag

Bilde Sätze im *present perfect* mit den folgenden Angaben.

Tom / be / to school. ______________________________

He / just / come back. ______________________________

His mum / be / shopping. ______________________________

She / buy a lot of things. ______________________________

She / do / the cooking. ______________________________

She / clean the bathroom. ______________________________

Tom / help her. ______________________________

They / have a busy day. ______________________________

They / do / a lot of things. ______________________________

281 ★★☆ Toms Vater

a) Bilde Sätze im *present perfect*.

Tom's father / be / very busy, too. ______________________________

He / leave the house. ______________________________

But he / not be in his office. ______________________________

He / not help his wife. ______________________________

He / be away on business. ______________________________

He / take the train to London. ______________________________

b) Wo stehen im *present perfect* die Ergänzungen zum Verb?

○ vor dem Partizip ○ hinter dem Partizip

280 Tom has been to school. He has just come back. His mum has been shopping. She has bought a lot of things. She has done the cooking. She has cleaned the bathroom. Tom has helped her. They have had a busy day. They have done a lot of things.

281 a) Tom's father has been very busy, too. He has left the house. But he has not been in his office. He has not helped his wife. He has been away on business. He has taken the train to London.
b) Sie stehen immer hinter dem Partizip.

282 ★★☆ Kurzantworten

Schaue dir die Kurztests 280 und 281 nochmals an und gib dann die entsprechenden Kurzantworten.

Has Tom been to school? ____________, ______________________________

Has he had a busy day? ____________, ______________________________

Has he helped his mother? ____________, ______________________________

Has his father helped, too? ____________, ______________________________

Has she been angry? ____________, ______________________________

Have they gone for a walk? ____________, ______________________________

Have they been to the cinema? ____________, ______________________________

Has Tom been ill? ____________, ______________________________

283 ★★☆ Fragen mit Fragewörtern

Bilde Fragen im *present perfect*.

Why he not help his wife? ______________________________?

Where Tom be? ______________________________?

Who he help? ______________________________?

Which rooms they clean? ______________________________?

Why she not be angry? ______________________________?

Where he be all day? ______________________________?

What they not do? ______________________________?

Who help her? ______________________________?

282 Yes, he has. Yes, he has. Yes, he has. No, he hasn't. No, she hasn't. No, they haven't. No, they haven't. No, he hasn't.

283 Why hasn't he helped his wife? Where has Tom been? Who has he helped? Which rooms have they cleaned? Why hasn't she been angry? Where has he been all day? What have they not done / haven't they done? Who has helped her?

284 ★★☆ In einem Reisebüro

Lies dir den folgenden Text durch und gib Kurzantworten.

Good afternoon. Have a seat, please. What can I do for you? *We'd like to book a holiday, but we haven't decided yet. I hope you can help us.* Okay, then let me ask you some questions first.

Have you ever been to Italy? No, ______________________.

Have you been to Spain yet? No, ______________________.

Haven't you been to Majorca yet? No, ______________________.

Have you already been to Wales? No, ______________________.

Have you always spent your holidays in GB? Yes, ______________________.

Have you never been abroad*? No, ______________________.

Okay, then have a look at this catalogue, please. It has just arrived.

* abroad = im Ausland

285 ★★☆ Signalwörter

Lies den letzten Kurztest erneut durch und schreibe die Signalwörter heraus, die mit dem *present perfect* stehen.

a) Was bedeuten sie auf Deutsch und b) wo stehen sie im Satz?

Signalwörter:	deutsche Bedeutung:
e ______________	______________
y ______________	______________
n ________ y ________	______________
a ______________	______________
a ______________	______________
n ______________	______________
j ______________	______________

b) yet: ______________ ever, never, already: ______________

284 No, we haven't. No, we haven't. No, we haven't. No, we haven't. Yes, we have. No, we haven't.
285 a) ever = jemals; yet = schon; not yet = noch nicht; already = schon, bereits; always = immer; never = noch nie, niemals; just = gerade. **b)** *yet* steht am Satzende; die Anderen wie *ever, never* stehen vor dem Partizip.

286 ★★☆ Urlaubsüberlegungen

Bilde Sätze mit den angegebenen Signalwörtern.

The Bensons / not be / on holiday. (this year)

____

They / take / their holiday. (not … yet)

____

They / decide / where they want to go this year. (not … yet)

____

They / spend their holidays in England. (always)

____

They / be to Wales or other parts of Great Britain. (never)

____

They / hear a lot about Wales. (already)

____

287 ★★☆ Fragen an dich

Bilde Fragen mit den angegebenen Signalwörter.

a) Have you been to England? (schon) ______________________________?

b) Have you been to London? (jemals) ______________________________?

c) Have you been abroad? (noch nicht) ______________________________?

d) Have you been to the US? (schon) ______________________________?

e) Have you wanted to go there? (nie) ______________________________?

286 The Bensons haven't been on holiday this year. They haven't taken their holiday yet. They haven't decided yet where they want to go this year. They have always spent their holidays in England. They have never been to Wales or other parts of Great Britain. They have already heard a lot about Wales.

287 a) Have you already been to England? **b)** Have you ever been to London? **c)** Haven't you been abroad yet? / Have you not been abroad yet? **d)** Have you been to the US yet? / Have you already been to the US? **e)** Have you never wanted to go there?

288 ★★☆ Was ich noch weiß

Schaue dir die Sätze genau an und beantworte dann die folgenden Fragen.

The Bensons will spend their holidays in Wales.

They have never been there. They have always spent their holidays in England.

Their tickets have just arrived. They have just opened the envelope.

a) Was für Handlungen drückt das *present perfect* aus? Wann haben sie begonnen? Wann sind sie vorbei?

____

b) Wie sieht es aus mit Handlungen, bei denen *just* (= gerade) steht? Wann sind sie zu Ende gegangen?

____

289 ★★☆ Was sie schon getan haben

Setze die folgenden Sätze in das *present perfect*.

1. They / buy a map. ____________________
2. They / plan their route. ____________________
3. They / clean their car. ____________________
4. They / prepare some sandwiches. ____________________
5. They / buy something to drink. ____________________
6. They / pack their bags. ____________________
7. They / have put their bags in the car. ____________________
8. They / lock the door. ____________________
9. They / leave a window open. ____________________

288 a) Das *present perfect* wird für Handlungen oder Zustände verwandt, die in der Vergangenheit begonnen haben und in die Gegenwart hineinreichen. **b)** Handlungen mit *just* sind kurz vor dem gegenwärtigen Zeitpunkt zu Ende gegangen. **Tipp:** Im amerikanischen Englisch wird hier meistens das *simple past* benutzt.
289 1. They have bought a map. **2.** They have planned their route. **3.** They have cleaned their car. **4.** They have prepared some sandwiches. **5.** They have bought something to drink. **6.** They have packed their bags. **7.** They have put their bags in the car. **8.** They have locked the door. **9.** They have left a window open.

290 ★★☆ Und was daraus wurde …

1. Ordne die folgenden Sätze den Sätzen im Kurztest 289 zu.

_____ a) It's locked.

_____ b) It's not dirty anymore.

_____ c) They can see which road to take.

_____ d) They are in the car now.

_____ e) The bottles are here.

_____ f) They know where to go.

_____ g) They can put them in the car.

_____ h) It's still open.

_____ i) They have something to eat.

2. Was drückt das *present perfect* in diesen Sätzen aus?

____

____

291 ★★☆ Bedeutungen

Vervollständige die Sätze mit den folgenden Verben:

kiss *see (2 x)* *come true* *have* *find* *leave* *do*

I know this film. I ____________________ it before.

Of course, I ____________________ my homework. Here it is.

Where is my textbook? Oh, no. I think I ____________________ it on the bus.

Where are my keys? ______________ you ____________________ them?

No, thank you. I'm not hungry. I ______________ just ____________ lunch.

Do you know where John and Alice are? No, I ____________________ them.

Look! There is lipstick on his face. Alice ____________________ him.

He's very happy. His dream ____________________.

290 1. a) 8; b) 3; c) 1; d) 7; e) 5; f) 2; g) 6; h) 9; i) 4 **2.** Das *present perfect* drückt aus, dass eine Handlung oder etwas, das in der Vergangenheit passiert ist, in der Gegenwart noch spürbar oder sichtbar ist.
291 I have seen it before. Of course, I have done my homework. I think I have left it on the bus. Have you found them? I have just had lunch. No, I haven't seen them. Alice has kissed him. His dream has come true.

292 ★★☆ Ein Sturm

Das *present perfect* oder das *simple past*?

While they __________ (be) on their way to Wales, a heavy storm ____________________ (hit) the area.

Luckily, they ___________ (be) in their car, but they ___________ (have) to stop under a bridge.

"Dear me," Mrs Benson ____________ (say) to her husband, "I ________________________ ________________ (never see) such a storm in all my life."

"We are lucky that we ____________________________ (not have) an accident."

Luckily, after an hour or so, they _____________________ (can) continue. When they finally _______________________ (arrive) at their hotel, it _______________ (be) sunny again.

293 ★★☆ Ein Bericht

a) Übersetze diesen Text. Pass auf, welche Zeit du nehmen musst.

Gestern sind wir um 8 Uhr abends angekommen. Wir haben unsere Koffer aus dem Wagen geholt und sind in das Hotel gegangen. Dort haben sie uns unsere Zimmer gezeigt. Wir haben dann ausgepackt. Danach haben wir ein Restaurant gesucht. Wir waren sehr hungrig.

____

____

____

b) Welche Zeit ist richtig und warum?

____

____

292 While they were on their way to Wales, a heavy storm hit the area. Luckily, they were in their car, but they had to stop under a bridge. „Dear me," Mrs Benson said to her husband, „I have never seen such a storm in all my life." We are lucky that we haven't had an accident." Luckily, after an hour or so, they could continue. When they finally arrived at their hotel, it was sunny again.

293 a) We arrived at 8 yesterday evening. We took our bags out of our car and went into the hotel. They showed us our rooms there. Then we unpacked our things. After that we looked for a restaurant. We were very hungry.
b) Du musst das *simple past* gebrauchen. Bei den obigen Sätzen handelt es sich um aufeinanderfolgende Handlungen.

294 ★★★ Hunger

Das *present perfect* oder das *simple past*? Setze die richtigen Zeiten ein.

Tom: I'm really hungry. You know we ____________________ (not stop) once the whole way, and we ____________________ (leave) this morning at about 8 o'clock.

Tom's father: I'm very hungry, too. I ____________________ (not eat) anything either.

Tom's mother: I ________________ (have) a sandwich this morning, but you ____________________ (not want) to eat any of them. At least, that's what you ____________________ (say) this morning. I ________________ (have) two sandwiches, so I'm not that hungry.

295 ★★★ Im Restaurant

Setze die richtigen Zeiten ein.

Tom's father: Waiter, can we have the menu, please?

Waiter: Here you are. I'm afraid, we don't have any fresh fish today. The weather (1.) ______________ (be) so bad this morning that the fisherman (2.) ____________________ (cannot) go out and fish. In fact, the fishermen (3.) ____________________ (not catch) any fish all week.

Tom's father: Have you got any sausages? What about eggs and peas?

Waiter: Sorry, we are out of everything. Nobody (4.) ____________________ (go) shopping this morning.

Tom's father: What kind of restaurant is this? With no food? Okay, then let's go to our hotel and eat Mum's old sandwiches. I hope you (5.) ____________________ already ____________________ (not throw) them away.

294 … we haven't stopped once …; … we left this morning …; … I haven't eaten anything either.; I had a sandwich this morning, but you didn't want to eat …; … what you said this morning. I had two …
295 **1.** was **2.** couldn't **3.** haven't caught **4.** went **5.** haven't already thrown

296 ★☆☆ Am nächsten Tag

Setze die Sätze in das *will-future*.

The Bensons / go for a walk. ______________________________

They / visit the old town. ______________________________

They / go down to the harbour. ______________________________

They / have a look at the boats. ______________________________

They / have lunch at a restaurant. ______________________________

Tom / send a text message* to a friend. ______________________________

Mr Benson / buy a newspaper. ______________________________

* text message = SMS (to text someone = jemandem eine SMS schreiben)

297 ★☆☆ Was sie nicht tun werden

Setze die folgenden Sätze in das *will-future*. Gebrauche die Langformen für Satz 1 bis 4, ab Satz 5 die Kurzformen.

1. They ______________________ (not get) up early.
2. They ______________________ (not stay) hungry all day.
3. Mrs Benson ______________________ (not prepare) any sandwiches.
4. They ______________________ (not eat) sandwiches.
5. They ______________________ (not go) to the same restaurant again.
6. They ______________________ (not have) lunch there.
7. Mrs Benson ______________________ (not do) any cooking.
8. She ______________________ (not stand) in the kitchen all day.
9. She ______________________ (not be) unhappy about it.

296 The Benson will go for a walk. They will visit the old town. The will go down to the harbour. They will have a look at the boats. They will have lunch at a restaurant. Tom will send a text message to a friend. Mr Benson will buy a newspaper.

297 1. They will not get up early. **2.** They will not stay hungry all day. **3.** Mrs Benson will not prepare any sandwiches. **4.** They will not eat sandwiches. **5.** They won't go to the same restaurant again. **6.** They won't have lunch there. **7.** Mrs Benson won't do any cooking. **8.** She won't stand in the kitchen all day. **9.** She won't be unhappy about it.

298 ★★☆ Ja oder nein?

Schaue dir die Kurztests 296 und 297 erneut an und gib dann Kurzantworten.

a) Will the Bensons go for a walk? ______________, ____________________.

b) Will they walk down to the harbour? ______________, ____________________.

c) Will they take their car? ______________, ____________________.

d) Will they have lunch at the same restaurant? ______________, ____________________.

e) Will Mrs Benson prepare sandwiches again? ______________, ____________________.

f) Will they eat sandwiches? ______________, ____________________.

g) Will Mrs Benson do the cooking? ______________, ____________________.

h) Will she be happy? ______________, ____________________.

i) Will they have lunch at a restaurant? ______________, ____________________.

299 ★★☆ Fragen über Fragen

Bilde Fragen im *will-future*.

The Bensons / find a nice restaurant? ________________________________

They / have to eat their old sandwiches? ________________________________

They / be happy about that? ________________________________

Fresh fish / be on the menu? ________________________________

They all / eat the same thing? ________________________________

They / enjoy the meal? ________________________________

They / pay for it? ________________________________

298 a) Yes, they will. **b)** Yes, they will. **c)** No, they won't. **d)** No, they won't. **e)** No, she won't. **f)** No, they won't. **g)** No, she won't. **h)** Yes, she will. **i)** Yes, they will.
299 Will the Bensons find a nice restaurant? Will they have to eat their old sandwiches? Will they be happy about that? Will fresh fish be on the menu? Will they all eat the same thing? Will they enjoy the meal? Will they pay for it?

300 ★★☆ Und wie wird das Wetter?

a) Setze die entsprechenden Formen des *will-future* ein.

Tomorrow the weather ________________________ better (be).

There ________________________ (not be) any rain in the morning.

There ________________________ (be) a lot of sunshine in the afternoon.

But in the evening it ________________ cloudy (be).

There ________________ (be) rain in some parts of the country.

Temperatures ________________ (be) around 20 °C in the afternoon.

b) Wovon hängen diese Handlungen bzw. Zustände ab?

Von dem, was die Bensons wollen oder wünschen oder von äußeren Bedingungen, die sie nicht beeinflussen können?

____

301 ★★☆ Und was glauben die Bensons?

a) Bilde Sätze im *will-future* mit den folgenden Angaben.

I think/it be pretty good today. ________________________

Probably/it be warmer later. ________________________

Probably/it not rain. ________________________

I hope/there not be a storm again. ________________________

I believe/it be rather windy, though*. ________________________

* though – jedoch

b) Was drücken Verben wie *I believe, I hope, I'm sure* aus?

____

300 a) … weather will be better. There won't be any rain … There will be a lot of sunshine … But in the evening it will be cloudy. There will be rain … Temperatures will be around 20 °C … **b)** Das *will-future* drückt u. a. aus, dass etwas unabhängig vom eigenen Wollen oder Hoffen in der Zukunft geschieht.

301 a) I think it will be pretty good today. Probably it will be warmer later. Probably it won't rain. I hope there won't be a storm again. I believe it will be rather windy, though. **b)** Diese Verben drücken eine Hoffnung oder Vermutung aus.

302 ★★☆ Was geschieht, wenn …

Bilde sinnvolle Sätze mit den folgenden Angaben.

If the weather is nice, the Bensons / go to the beach

____

If it rains, the Bensons / stay at their hotel

____

If they can find an umbrella, they / go for a walk

____

If it's hot, the Bensons / not go out

____

If there is a storm again, they / not rent a boat

____

303 ★★☆ Wenn Tom nach Hause kommt …

a) Bilde sinnvolle Sätze.

When Tom ______________ home (come), he ______________ his friends (see).

When Tom ______________ them (see), he ______________ happy (be).

When he ______________ them (see), he ______________ them about his holidays (tell).

When Tom ______________ them his stories (tell), they ______________ (laugh).

b) In welchem Satzteil steht in den vorigen Sätzen das *will-future*? In welchem Satzteil steht das Präsens?

____

302 If the weather is nice, the Bensons will go to the beach. If it rains, the Bensons will stay at their hotel. If they can find an umbrella, they will go for a walk. If it's hot, the Bensons won't go out. If there is a storm again, they won't rent a boat.
303 a) When Tom comes home, he will see his friends. When Tom sees them, he will be happy. When he sees them, he will tell them about his holidays. When Tom tells them his stories, they will laugh.
b) Das *will-future* steht im Hauptsatz, das Präsens im Nebensatz.

304 ★★☆ Zusammenfassung

Ordne die Beispielsätze den passenden „Regeln“ für das *will-future* zu.

Das *will-future* gebraucht man

_____ 1) The weather will be nice tomorrow.

_____ 2) If the weather is nice tomorrow, we will go to the beach.

_____ 3) I think it will be warmer later.

a) um Vermutungen und Hoffnungen auszudrücken.

b) für zukünftige Handlungen und Ereignisse, die nicht vom Wollen des Sprechers abhängen.

c) in Nebensätzen der Zeit und der Bedingung, wenn sie sich auf die Zukunft beziehen.

305 ★★★ *When* und *if*

a) Schaue dir diese Sätze an. Bei welchen Sätzen ist die Handlung sicher oder wahrscheinlich?

1) When Tom comes, he will help you.

2) If Tom comes, he will help you.

When bezieht sich auf einen Zeitpunkt, zu dem etwas geschieht oder geschehen wird (when = wenn). *If* drückt dagegen eine Annahme oder Möglichkeit aus (if = falls).

b) Setze *when* oder *if* ein.

1) What will the Bensons do _____________ there is another tornado?

(Tornados sind selten.)

2) What will Tom do _____________ he gets home?

(Tom wird in 2 Stunden nach Hause kommen.)

3) What will he do _____________ there is no more food?

(Es ist Samstag, 20 Uhr und der Supermarkt ist fast leer gekauft.)

4) Will Tom be happy _____________ he sees his friend again?

(Seine Freundin wird am nächsten Tag aus dem Urlaub zurückkommen.)

304 1) b; **2)** c; **3)** a

305 a) Satz 1 ist sicher oder wahrscheinlich. **b) 1)** if; **2)** when; **3)** when; **4)** when

306 ★☆☆ Die Bildung des *going to-future*

Vervollständige die Formen.

I am going to go home.

He ____________________

She ____________________

We ____________________

You ____________________

They ____________________

I am not going to go home.

He ____________________

She ____________________

We ____________________

You ____________________

They ____________________

307 ★☆☆ Was sie tun wollen

Setze die Sätze in das *going to-future*.

Mr Benson / read all the old papers. ____________________

He / watch a football match. ____________________

After that he / clean his car. ____________________

Mrs Benson / not help her husband. ____________________

She / go shopping. ____________________

She / buy a birthday present. ____________________

Tom / call Debbie. ____________________

He / have a long talk with her. ____________________

They / not talk about school. ____________________

They / talk about their holidays. ____________________

306 He is going to go home. She is going to go home. We are going to go home. You are going to go home. They are going to go home.; He is not going to go home. She is not going to go home. We are not going to go home. You are not going to go home. They are not going to go home.

307 Mr Benson is going to read all the old papers. He is going to watch a football match. After that he is going to clean his car. Mrs Benson is not going to help her husband. She is going to go shopping. She is going to buy a birthday present. Tom is going to call Debbie. He is going to have a long talk with her. They are not going to talk about school. They are going to talk about their holidays.

308 ★★☆ Feste Absichten und Pläne

Das Schuljahr beginnt bald wieder. Manche Kinder haben für das neue Schuljahr gute Vorsätze gefasst. Hier sind sie. Mache ganze Sätze daraus.

Tom / not sleep so much

Mike and Ken / not talk so much

Ian / do his homework

Kevin / leave the girls alone

Debbie / work harder

Fiona and Sue / not be late to class anymore

Alice / not forget her homework

John / not drive his teachers crazy

____

____

____

____

____

____

____

____

____

____

309 ★★☆ Nachgefragt

Ergänze, was fehlt.

1) What are you going to do, Tom? Are you going to work more?

No, I ______________, but ______________________________ so much.

2) And what about you, Mike? Are you going to talk less?

Yes, ______________. I'm not ______________________________ so much.

3) And what about you, Fiona and Sue? Are you going to work harder?

No, ______________, but we ______________________________ to class anymore.

4) And, Ian? What about you? Are you going to do your homework?

Yes, ______________. ______________________________ everyday.

308 Tom isn't going to sleep so much. Mike and Ken aren't going to talk so much. Ian is going to do his homework. Kevin is going to leave the girls alone. Debbie is going to work harder. Fiona and Sue are not going to be late to class anymore. Alice is not going to forget her homework. John isn't going to drive his teachers crazy.
309 1) No, I'm not, but I am not going to sleep so much. **2)** Yes, I am. I'm not going to talk so much. **3)** No, we aren't, but we are not going to be late to class anymore. **4)** Yes, I am. I'm going to do my homework everyday.

310 ★★☆ Fragen an dich

Bilde die Fragen und gib Kurzantworten.

1) You / work harder this term?

_______________________________________? ______, __________.

2) You / study more for your tests?

_______________________________________? ______, __________.

3) You / get better marks*?

_______________________________________? ______, __________.

4) You / watch less TV?

_______________________________________? ______, __________.

5) Your friends / help you?

_______________________________________? ______, __________.

* marks (AmE: grades) = Schulnoten (NICHT "notes"! Falsche Freunde!)

311 ★★☆ Fragen mit Fragewörtern

Bilde fünf sinnvolle Fragen mit den folgenden Substantiven, Pronomen und Verben:

Subjects: your parents, Debbie, you, your friends, Alice, Tom, he

Verbs: buy, call, come, see, do, meet, visit

What _______________________________________?

Why _______________________________________?

When _______________________________________?

Who _______________________________________?

Where _______________________________________?

310 1) Are you going to work harder this term? Yes, I am. / No, I'm not. **2)** Are you going to study more for your tests? Yes, I am. / No, I'm not. **3)** Are you going to get better marks? Yes, I am. / No, I'm not. **4)** Are you going to watch less TV? Yes, I am. / No, I'm not. **5)** Are your friends going to help you? Yes, they are. / No, they aren't.

311 Mögliche Antworten: What are your parents going to buy? Why are you going to call him? When are your friends going to visit us? Who is Debbie going to meet? Where is Tom going to meet her?

312 ★★★ Was weißt du noch?

Das **going to-future** bezieht sich auf die Zukunft; es wird für zukünftige feste Pläne und Absichten gebraucht.

Das **will-future** wird gebraucht,
a) wenn man ausdrücken will, dass etwas unabhängig vom eigenen Wollen in der Zukunft geschieht;
b) für Hoffnungen und Vermutungen;
c) im Hauptsatz, wenn der Nebensatz eine Bedingung oder eine Annahme enthält, die sich auf die Zukunft bezieht.

1) I think he will be there, but I'm not sure. ○ richtig ○ falsch

2) We're going to be there tomorrow. I promise! ○ richtig ○ falsch

3) I don't care what he says! I am going to watch TV tonight. ○ richtig ○ falsch

313 ★★★ Debbies Geburtstagsparty

Setze das *going to-* oder das *will-future* ein. Vergiss nicht das *to*!

a) This year Debbie ______________________ be twelve.

b) She ______________________ have a big party.

c) She ______________________ invite all her friends.

d) She is sure that her parents ______________________ let her have the party.

e) She hopes that all her friends ______________________ come.

f) She hopes that it ______________________ not rain.

g) If it doesn't rain, they ______________________ be able to play in the garden.

h) She doesn't know yet when everyone ______________________ arrive.

i) She ______________________ buy some lemonade, some coke and a lot of crisps*.

j) She ______________________ get* some sausages and some ice-cream, too.

k) She believes that everybody ______________________ like that.

* crisps (AmE: chips) = Kartoffelchips (**Tipp!** Im Britischen heißt "chips" Pommes!)
** to get = holen (nicht nur „bekommen")

312 1) richtig **2)** richtig **3)** richtig
313 a) will **b)** is going to **c)** is going to **d)** will **e)** will **f)** will **g)** will **h)** will **i)** is going to **j)** is going to **k)** will

314 ★★☆ Ein Überblick

Setze die Verben in die entsprechenden Zeiten.

a) Debbie ______________________________ back. (be – present)

b) She ______________________________ back. (just come – present perfect)

c) She ______________________________ little time. (have got – present)

d) She ______________________________ her things. (unpack – pres. progressive)

e) She ______________________ go to school on Monday. (have to – present)

f) She ______________________ in Majorca with Mum. (be – past)

g) She ______________________________ go with her. (must – past)

h) She ______________________________ stay home. (mustn't – past)

i) But she ______________________ her stay anyway. (enjoy – past)

j) She ______________________________ on the beach. (can lie – past)

k) They ______________________________ there again. (go – going to-future)

l) The next time ______________________ fun, too! (be – will-future)

315 ★★☆ Was entspricht wem?

Welche Zeiten entsprechen diesen Bildungsregeln? Trage sie ein.

Subjekt + be + present participle = ______________________________

S + have + past participle = ______________________________

S + infinitive + (e)s in der 3. Person sing. = ______________________________

S + infinitive + -ed / irreg. form = ______________________________

S + will + infinitive = ______________________________

S + be + going to + infinitive = ______________________________

314 a) is **b)** has just come **c)** has got **d)** is unpacking **e)** has to **f)** was **g)** had to **h)** wasn't allowed to **i)** enjoyed **j)** could lie **k)** are going to go **l)** will be
315 present oder past progressive, present perfect, simple present, simple past, will-future, going to-future

316 ★★☆ Was passiert mit dem *y*?

Nach Vokal bleibt es immer erhalten, aber wie steht es

1) in der 3. Person Sing. Präsens nach Konsonanten?

try he ______ carry she ______

fly it ______ hurry he ______

2) im *simple past* nach Konsonanten?

try he ______ hurry he ______

carry she ______ worry they ______

3) im *past participle* nach Konsonanten?

try ______ hurry ______

carry ______ worry ______

4) mit der Pluralbildung und mit den Steigerungsformen von Adjektiven?

one baby – two ______ one party – three ______

schön – schöner – am schönsten = pretty – ______ – the ______

317 ★★☆ Schreibungen

Wie bildest du das *present participle* von

a) see ______ agree ______

b) take ______ come ______

give ______ use ______

c) die ______ lie ______

d) drop ______ swim ______

stop ______ run ______

316 1) he tries, she carries, it flies, he hurries; **2)** he tried, he hurried, she carried, they worried; **3)** tried, hurried, carried, worried, **4)** two babies, three parties; pretty – prettier – the prettiest

317 a) seeing, agreeing; **b)** taking, coming, giving, using; **c)** dying, lying; **d)** dropping, swimming, stopping, running

318 ★★☆ Fragen

Stelle Fragen.

Yes, she is back. ______________________________?

Yes, she has just come back. ______________________________?

No, she hasn't got much time. ______________________________?

She is unpacking her things. ______________________________?

She feels fine. ______________________________?

Yes, she can go back to school. ______________________________?

She was in Majorca with her parents. ______________________________?

Yes, she enjoyed her stay very much. ______________________________?

Yes, she could lie on the beach. ______________________________?

Yes, they are going to go back again. ______________________________?

The weather will be fine. ______________________________?

319 ★★☆ Fragen zur Zeitenbildung

Sieh dir den vorigen Kurztest nochmal an und beantworte dann folgende Fragen:

1) Bei welchen Zeiten musst du in der Frage *to do* gebrauchen?

____

2) Was folgt nach den Formen von *to do*?

____

3) Wie wird die Frage bei den anderen Zeiten oder Verbformen gebildet?

____

318 Is Debbie back? Has she just come back? Has she got much time? Is she unpacking her things? How does she feel? Can she go back to school? Where was she? Did she enjoy her stay? Could she lie on the beach? Are they going to go back again? How will the weather be?

319 1) Im *simple present* und im *simple past* (Vollverben) **2)** Nach den Formen von *to do* folgt immer der Infinitiv. **3)** Durch Umstellung von Subjekt und Prädikat. (z. B. He is over there. – Is he over there?) In der Frage steht der erste Teil des Prädikats vor dem Subjekt.

320 ★★☆ Fragen nach dem Subjekt

Stelle Fragen nach dem Subjekt.

The Wilsons have come back. ______________________________ ?

Debbie has gone to school again. ______________________________ ?

Her mother doesn't feel well. ______________________________ ?

Debbie feels sad. ______________________________ ?

Debbie and her mother aren't happy. ______________________________ ?

Their holidays are over. ______________________________ ?

Mrs Wilson enjoyed the holidays. ______________________________ ?

Mrs Wilson didn't want to come back. ______________________________ ?

Debbie's books are lying on the floor. ______________________________ ?

Debbie is going to go there again. ______________________________ ?

321 ★★☆ Das solltest du jetzt wissen ...

Finde die richtige Antwort. Manchmal sind mehrere Antworten richtig.

a) Bei Fragen nach dem Subjekt gebrauchst du: ● what ● who ● how.

b) Das folgende Verb steht danach immer im: ● Singular ● Plural.

c) Bei Fragen nach dem Subjekt darfst du im *simple present* oder im *simple past to do* nur in: ● verneinten ● nicht verneinten Fragen gebrauchen.

d) Bei Fragen nach allen anderen Satzteilen steht im *simple present* und *simple past* immer die entsprechende Form von: ● to be ● to do.

320 Who has come back? Who has gone to school again? Who doesn't feel well? Who feels sad? Who isn't happy? What is over? Who enjoyed the holidays? Who didn't want to come back? What is lying on the floor? Who is going to go there again?
321 a) Bei Fragen nach dem Subjekt gebrauchst du *who* oder *what*. **b)** Das folgende Verb steht danach immer im Singular. **c)** Bei Fragen nach dem Subjekt darfst du im *simple present* oder im *simple past to do* nur in nicht verneinten Fragen gebrauchen. **d)** Bei Fragen nach anderen Satzteilen steht im *simple present* und im *simple past* immer die entsprechende Form von *to do*.

322 ★★☆ Aber es gibt auch gute Dinge …

Frage nach den hervorgehobenen Satzteilen.

She can see **her friends** again. ______________________________?

They are waiting for her. ______________________________?

She will see them **in a few days.** ______________________________?

They are going to talk about **their holidays.** ______________________________?

She can see **Tom.** ______________________________?

She likes **him.** ______________________________?

She knows **that he likes her.** ______________________________?

They can **play tennis** together. ______________________________?

323 ★★☆ Frag Debbie

Gib Kurzantworten.

1) Did you enjoy your holidays? Yes, ______________________________.

2) Where were you? Were you in Majorca? Yes, ______________________________.

3) Are you unhappy now? No, ______________________________.

4) Do you feel sad? Yes, ______________________________.

5) Do you want to go to school again? No, ______________________________.

6) Have you already packed your things? No, ______________________________.

7) Can I come to see you? Yes, ______________________________.

8) Have you seen Tom yet? No, ______________________________.

9) Are you going to see him tomorrow? Yes, ______________________________.

10) Will that make you happy? Yes, ______________________________.

322 Who can she see again? Who is waiting for her? When will she see them? What are they going to talk about? Who can she see? Who does she like? What does she know? What can they do together?
323 1) Yes, I did. **2)** Yes, I was. **3)** No, I'm not. **4)** Yes, I do. **5)** No, I don't. **6)** No, I haven't. **7)** Yes, you can. **8)** No, I haven't. **9)** Yes, I am. **10)** Yes, it will.

324 ★★☆ Ende gut, alles gut

Setze die folgenden Sätze in die Verneinung.

1) Debbie ______________ feel unhappy anymore. (feel: present)

2) She ______________ crying anymore. (cry: present progressive)

3) She ______________ unhappy anymore. (must be: present)

4) She ______________ unhappy yesterday. (be: past)

5) She ______________ lonely. (be: present)

6) Her friends ______________ her once. (write: present perfect)

7) I hope they ______________ her. (forget: present perfect)

8) She ______________ them, I'm sure. (forget: will-future)

9) She ______________ Tom for a long time. (see: present perfect)

10) He ______________ her, I'm sure. (call: will-future)

11) But it ______________ now. (matter: present)

325 ★★☆ Das weißt du doch jetzt sicher auch ...

Wie sieht es mit der Verneinung aus? Kannst du die richtigen Antworten für die folgenden Fragen finden?

1) Im *simple present* und im *simple past* wird die Verneinung mit gebildet. ● to be ● to do

2) Darauf folgt ● der Infinitiv ● das *past participle*

3) Bei allen anderen Zeiten und Verbformen wird die Verneinung mit gebildet. ● not ● no

Es gelten damit die selben Regeln wie für die Fragebildung.

324 1) doesn't feel **2)** isn't crying **3)** needn't be **4)** wasn't **5)** isn't **6)** haven't written **7)** haven't forgotten **8)** won't forget **9)** hasn't seen **10)** won't call **11)** doesn't matter

325 1) Im *simple present* und im *simple past* wird die Verneinung mit *to do* gebildet. **2)** Das folgende Verb steht im Infinitiv. **3)** Bei allen anderen Zeiten und Verbformen wird die Verneinung mit *not* gebildet.

326 ★★☆ Debbie

Ergänze den richtigen *question tag*.

Debbie is a nice girl, ______________________?

She has got many friends, ______________________?

Many people like her, ______________________?

You like her, too, ______________________?

She likes Tom, ______________________?

She will see him soon, ______________________?

She isn't still unhappy, ______________________?

You could see it, ______________________?

She didn't feel well yesterday, ______________________?

But she wasn't ill, ______________________?

There was no need to worry, ______________________?

327 ★★☆ Bestätigungsfragen

Beantworte die folgenden Fragen.

1) Handelt es sich bei Bestätigungsfragen um richtige Fragen?

● ja ● nein

2) Woran werden sie angehängt?

● an die Frage ● an den Aussagesatz

3) Sind sie positiv, wenn der vorausgehende Satz negativ ist und umgekehrt?

● ja ● nein

4) Gelten für ihre Bildung dieselben Regeln wie für Kurzantworten?

● ja ● nein

326 … isn't she?, … hasn't she?, … don't they?, … don't you?, … doesn't she?, … won't she?, … is she?, … couldn't you?, … did she?, … was she?, … was there?

327 1) nein **2)** an den Aussagesatz **3)** ja **4)** ja

328 ★☆☆ Bildung

Bilde die Adverbien der folgenden Adjektive.

bad ____________________ slow ____________________

quick ____________________ quiet ____________________

nervous ____________________ dangerous ____________________

stupid ____________________ excited ____________________

careful ____________________ beautiful ____________________

nice ____________________ complete ____________________

329 ★★☆ Und wie sieht es hier aus?

Bilde die Adverbien der folgenden Adjektive.

noisy ____________________ lazy ____________________

terrible ____________________ simple ____________________

horrible ____________________ fast ____________________

hard ____________________ good ____________________

330 ★★☆ Wie schreibst du die folgenden Adverbien?

Ergänze die fehlenden Buchstaben.

a) awfu____y, crue____y, gratefu____y, officia____y, rea____y, usefu____y

b) larg____ly, nic____ly, saf____ly, polit____ly, strang____ly, aggressiv____ly

c) bus____ly, craz____ly, luck____ly, happ____ly, nois____ly

328 badly, quickly, nervously, stupidly, carefully, nicely; slowly, quietly, dangerously, excitedly, beautifully, completely

329 noisily, terribly, horribly, hard; lazily, simply, fast, well

330 a) awfully, cruelly, gratefully, officially, really, usefully; **b)** largely, nicely, safely, politely, strangely, aggressively; **c)** busily, crazily, luckily, happily, noisily

331 ★★☆ Was weißt du noch?

Beantworte die folgenden Fragen.

a) Wie bildest du das Adverb von Adjektiven im Normalfall? Was hängt man an die Grundform des Adjektivs an? ______________________

b) Bei welchen Adjektiven musst du aufpassen, wenn du das Adverb bildest?

Bei Adjektiven, die auf ____________, ____________, und ____________ enden.

c) Welche drei Adverbien haben unregelmäßige Formen?

____

332 ★★☆ Wie sie sind, so handeln sie …

Setze die entsprechenden Adverbien ein.

Sam is a slow learner.	He learns ____________.
Ken isn't a quick worker.	He doesn't work ____________.
Tom is a fast learner.	He learns ____________.
Mike has got a terrible voice.	He sings ____________.
Fiona has a beautiful handwriting.	She writes ____________.
Debbie is an intelligent girl.	She answers questions ____________.
Robert is a dangerous driver.	He drives ____________.
John is a very noisy boy.	He always runs around ____________.
Alice is a quiet girl.	She does everything ____________.
Joe's German is not good.	He doesn't speak German ____________.
Bob is a hard worker.	He always works ____________.

331 a) Ich hänge an die Grundform des Adjektivs ein *-ly* an. **b)** Bei Adjektiven, die auf *-e*, Konsonant + *-le* und *-ly* enden. **c)** good, fast, hard

332 He learns slowly. He doesn't work quickly. He learns fast. He sings terribly. She writes beautifully. She answers questions intelligently. He drives dangerously. He always runs around noisily. She does everything quietly. He doesn't speak German well. He works hard.

333 ★★☆ Steigerungsformen

Ergänze die fehlenden Formen.

Grundform	Komparativ	Superlativ
quickly	______	______
angrily	______	______
slowly	______	______
quietly	______	______
nervously	______	______
carefully	______	______
dangerously	______	______
terribly	______	______
politely	______	______

334 ★★☆ Und wie steht es mit diesen Adverbien?

Ergänze die fehlenden Formen.

Grundform	Komparativ	Superlativ
hard	______	______
fast	______	______
well	______	______
badly	______	______
much (= sehr)	______	______

333 quickly, more quickly, most quickly; angrily, more angrily, most angrily; slowly, more slowly, most slowly; quietly, more quietly, most quietly; nervously, more nervously, most nervously; carefully, more carefully, most carefully; dangerously, more dangerously, most dangerously; terribly, more terribly, most terribly; politely, more politely, most politely

334 hard, harder, hardest; fast, faster, fastest; well, better, best; badly, worse, worst; much, more, most

335 ★★☆ I'm the greatest!

Setze das entsprechende Adverb ein.

I've got a beautiful voice. I sing ______________________.

I'm a careful driver. I drive ______________________.

I'm a good tennis player. I play tennis ______________________.

I'm a fast swimmer. I swim ______________________.

I'm a hard worker. I work ______________________.

I always give intelligent answers. I always answer questions ______________________.

I'm an excellent dancer. I dance ______________________.

336 ★★☆ Manche können es besser ...

Bilde Sätze mit den folgenden Angaben.

Beispiel: John runs fast. Mike + / Ken ++

John runs fast. Mike runs faster, but Ken runs fastest.

1) Ken likes Alice very much. Ben + / John ++

____

2) Tom sings well. Bob + / Robert ++

____

3) Mike speaks German badly. John + / Kevin ++

____

4) Sue works hard. Alice + / Kate ++

____

335 I sing beautifully. I drive carefully. I play tennis well. I swim fast. I work hard. I always answer questions intelligently. I dance excellently.

336 1) Ken likes Alice very much. Ben likes her more, but John likes her most.
2) Tom sings well. Bob sings better, but Robert sings best.
3) Mike speaks German badly. John speaks it worse, but Kevin speaks it worst.
4) Sue works hard. Alice works harder, but Kate works hardest.

337 ★★☆ Debbie und Tom

a) Setze *(not) as ... as* oder *than* und die entsprechenden Formen des Adverbs ein.

Tom's German is quite good, but he doesn't speak German (1) ______________________

Debbie. She speaks German much (2) ______________________ Tom.

Tom's voice isn't bad, but Debbie sings (3) ______________________ Tom.

Debbie is a fast swimmer, but she doesn't swim (4) ______________________ he does.

Debbie is good at sports, but Tom can run (5) ______________________ she can.

Both play tennis, but Debbie doesn't play it (6) ____________ elegantly ____________ Tom.

Tom is a hard worker, but Debbie works (7) ______________________ he does.

b) Wann musst du die Grundform des Adverbs, wann den Komparativ gebrauchen?

____

____

338 ★★☆ Und die anderen ...

Ergänze, was fehlt.

a) Mike is a **fast** learner, but there are others who learn ______________________ he does.

b) Kevin is a **careful** worker. He works much ______________________ Mike.

c) Alice is a **clever** girl, but she doesn't answer ______________________ Debbie.

d) Joe's handwriting is **bad**. He writes even* ______________________ Fiona.

e) John isn't a **calm** boy. Others do things much ______________________ he does.

f) Ken doesn't learn things **easily**. He doesn't learn things ______________________ Tom.

* even worse = noch schlimmer; even better = noch besser

337 a) (1) as well as **(2)** better than **(3)** better than **(4)** as fast as **(5)** faster than **(6)** as elegantly as **(7)** harder than
b) Bei *(not) as ... as ...* steht die Grundform des Adverbs. Bei *than* steht immer der Komparativ.
338 a) faster than **b)** much more carefully than **c)** as cleverly as **d)** worse than **e)** much more calmly than **f)** as easily as Tom.

339 ★★☆ Weißt du noch?

Ergänze die Lücken.

1) Adjektive beziehen sich immer auf ein __________ oder __________.
Vor einem __________ steht daher nie ein Adverb.

2) Adverbien der Art und Weise geben an, wie etwas getan wird. Sie beziehen sich daher immer auf ein __________.

3) Ist das Verb *to be*, steht immer ein __________. Dies gilt jedoch nicht für die *progressive forms* (He is driving carefully).

340 ★★★ Eine seltsame Geschichte

Adjektiv oder Adverb? Setze die richtigen Formen ein.

Tom was lying __________ (quiet) in his bed when __________ (sudden) the door bell rang. Who could it be at that time? It was already rather __________ (late) and he was __________ (alone) in the house. Was he __________ (afraid)? No, he wasn't. He __________ (quick) got up and opened the door. Outside it was __________ (dark) and __________ (cold). He looked around __________ (careful), but he couldn't see anybody. He __________ (slow) went back to his room and to bed again. A minute later he heard the bell again. __________ (angry) he ran down to open the door, but he couldn't see anybody again. There was only a __________ (small) noise near the garden wall. Was somebody playing a __________ (dirty) trick on him?

339 1) ein Substantiv oder ein Pronomen / Substantiv **2)** Verb **3)** Adjektiv
340 quietly / suddenly / late / alone / afraid / quickly / dark and cold / carefully / slowly / Angrily / small / dirty

341 ★★☆ Ein schöner Tag

Übersetze die Sätze.

Heute bin ich krank.

Heute kann ich im Bett bleiben.

Heute muss ich nicht früh aufstehen.

Heute habe ich Fieber.

Wenn ich krank bin, kann ich zu Hause bleiben.

Heute bin ich glücklich.

342 ★★☆ Wo steht im Englischen das Subjekt?

Kreuze bitte an, was richtig ist.

1. Im Aussagesatz steht das Subjekt im Englischen immer
   - vor dem Verb
   - nach dem Verb
2. Steht vor dem Subjekt ein anderer Satzteil,
   - wird wie im Deutschen umgestellt
   - wird nicht umgestellt
3. Die Wortstellung Subjekt (S) Verb (V) gilt
   - auch für Nebensätze
   - nicht bei Nebensätzen

341 Today I am ill. Today I can stay in bed. Today I needn't get up early. Today I have a temperature. When I am ill, I can stay at home. Today I am happy.
342 1) vor dem Verb **2)** es wird nicht umgestellt **3)** gilt auch für Nebensätze

343 ★★☆ Vor dem Wiedersehen

Wie lauten diese Sätze richtig?

a) Yesterday / didn't / Debbie / feel well.

____

b) But today / feels better / Debbie.

____

c) Tom / she / can see / today / again.

____

d) At 8.30 / is going to / at school / be / she.

____

e) So / will have / they / enough time / to see each other.

____

344 ★★☆ Was werden sie tun?

Bilde 5 Sätze mit den folgenden Angaben. Beginne mit dem Nebensatz.

When they see each other

not cry *not talk about school* *laugh a lot* *have fun together* *be happy*

When they ____

____

____

____

____

343 a) Yesterday Debbie didn't feel well. **b)** But today Debbie feels better. **c)** Today she can see Tom again./ She can see Tom again today. **d)** She is going to be at school at 8.30./At 8.30 she is going to be at school. **e)** So they will have enough time to see each other.
344 When they see each other, they won't cry./… they won't talk about school./… they will laugh a lot./ … they will have fun together./… they will be happy.

345 ★★☆ Bald geht es wieder los ...

Stelle Fragen.

The children are back. ____?

Two children are ill. ____?

They can't come. ____?

They caught a cold yesterday. ____?

The teachers are there, too. ____?

Lessons will begin soon. ____?

A teacher is coming. ____?

The classroom door opens. ____?

The pupils stand up. ____?

346 ★★☆ Wo steht das Subjekt bei Fragen?

Markiere jeweils die richtige Aussage.

1) Bei dem *present* und *past* von *to be* steht das Subjekt

- a) vor den Formen von *to be*.
- b) nach den Formen von *to be*.

2) Bei einem Prädikat, das aus zwei Teilen besteht (z. B. *will be*) steht das Subjekt

- a) nach dem ersten Teil des Prädikats.
- b) am Satzanfang.

3) Dies gilt auch bei Fragen nach dem Subjekt.

- a) richtig
- b) falsch

4) Bei Fragen nach dem Subjekt ist die Wortstellung: *Who / what* + Verb.

- a) richtig
- b) falsch

345 Are the children back? Are two children ill? Can't they come? Did they catch a cold yesterday? Are the teachers there, too? Will lessons begin soon? Is a teacher coming? Does the classroom door open? Do the pupils stand up?

346 1) a) vor diesen Formen **2)** b) nach dem ersten Teil des Prädikats **3)** b) falsch **4)** a) richtig

347 ★★☆ Ein Neubeginn

Stelle Fragen nach dem hervorgehobenen Teil des Satzes.

A teacher enters the classroom. ____________________?

He is **new**. ____________________?

He says **hello**. ____________________?

He **tells** them his name. ____________________?

He asks for **their names**. ____________________?

He tries to learn **their names**. ____________________?

They sing a song. ____________________?

They play **a game**. ____________________?

They like **him**. ____________________?

348 ★★☆ Nach dem Unterricht

Wie lauten die Fragen richtig?

When / they / home / can / go? ____________________?

What / after school / do / do / they? ____________________?

Where / they / do / go? ____________________?

Why / John / doesn't / home / go? ____________________?

What / he / do / is going to? ____________________?

Who / Tom / has / seen? ____________________?

Where / he / is? ____________________?

What / he / doing / is? ____________________?

347 Who enters the classroom? What is he? What does he say? What does he do? What does he ask for? What does he try to learn? Who sings a song? What do they play? Who do they like?

348 When can they go home? What do they do after school? Where do they go? Why doesn't John go home? What is he going to do? Who has seen Tom? Where is he? What is he doing?

349 ★★☆ Wo ist Tom?

a) Übersetze die folgenden Sätze.

Hast du **Tom** gesehen?

____?

Ich kann **ihn** nicht finden.

____

Ja, ich habe **ihn** gesehen.

____

Als ich ihn sah, hat er **Debbie** gesucht.

____

Er hat auch **eine CD** gesucht.

____

b) Wo steht im Englischen das Objekt? Wo steht es im Deutschen?

____

350 ★★☆ German English …

Wie lauten die Sätze richtig?

I have him just seen. ____

He will to Debbie's house again go. ____

He will the house again leave. ____

He has something forgotten. ____

He must for it look. ____

He will it find. ____

349 a) Have you seen Tom? I can't find him. Yes, I have seen him. When I saw him, he was looking for Debbie. He was looking for a CD, too. **b)** Im Englischen stehen Objekte immer nach dem Verb oder der Verbgruppe. Im Deutschen trennt man Hilfsverb + Verb-Konstruktionen, sodass ein Objekt immer dazwischen liegt.

350 I have just seen him. He will go to Debbie's house again. He will leave the house again. He has forgotten something. He must look for it. He will find it.

351 ★★☆ Toms Freizeitkalender

Schreibe auf, was Tom tun will.

Monday	clean my bike	*On Monday, he's going to clean his bike.*
Tuesday	study for a test	
Wednesday	play table tennis	
Thursday	see Debbie	
Friday	practice playing the guitar	
Saturday	watch a football match on TV	
Sunday	go to the cinema with Debbie	

352 ★★☆ Deine Pläne

a) Sage, was du tun willst. Gebrauche dabei die folgenden Zeitangaben:

tonight *on Monday* *next week* *this summer* *in July* *this school year*

______________________________ (learn French)

______________________________ (stay in bed)

______________________________ (go to a pop concert)

______________________________ (work more)

______________________________ (go on holidays)

______________________________ (go to Spain)

b) Wo stehen Zeitangaben im Englischen? Sie stehen entweder am

______________ oder ______________.

351 On Tuesday he's going to study for a test. On Wednesday he is going to play table tennis. On Thursday, he is going to see Debbie. On Friday, he is going to practice playing the guitar. On Sunday he is going to watch a football match on TV. On Sunday he is going to go to the cinema with Debbie.

352 a) Mögliche Lösungen: Tonight I'm going to learn French. On Monday I'm going to stay in bed. Next week I'm going to go to a pop concert. This school year I'm going to work more. This summer I'm going to go on holidays. In July I'm going to go to Spain. **b)** Sie stehen entweder am Satzanfang oder am Satzende.

353 ★★☆ Ortsangaben

a) Unterstreiche die Ortsangaben und bilde Sätze.

There / near Tom's school / a park / is. ______________________________

He / there / often / goes. ______________________________

It's not very far. He / can / there / walk. ______________________________

There's / in the park / a playground. ______________________________

They / can / in the park / play. ______________________________

b) Wo stehen Ortsangaben zumeist im Englischen? ______________________________

c) Wo können sie sonst noch stehen? ______________________________

354 ★★☆ Das englische Schulsystem

a) Bilde Sätze mit den folgenden Angaben.

1) pupils / start school / when they are five / in England

____

2) to a comprehensive school / most English pupils / when they are eleven / go

____

3) they / can / when they are 16 / leave school

____

4) in most schools / at 8.30 / lessons start

____

b) Wenn in einem Satz Orts- und Zeitangaben zusammentreffen, wie ist dann die Reihenfolge? ______________________________

353 a) Near Tom's school there is a park. / There is a park near Tom's school.; He often goes there.; It's not very far. He can walk there.; There's a playground in the park.; They can play in the park.
b) am Satzende **c)** am Satzanfang

354 a) 1) In England pupils start school when they are five. / Pupils start school in England when they are five. **2)** Most English pupils go to a comprehensive school when they are eleven. / When they are eleven, most English pupils go to a comprehensive school. **3)** They can leave school when they are 16. / When they are 16, they can leave school. **4)** In most schools lessons start at 8.30. / Lessons start in most schools at 8.30. **b)** Die Reihenfolge ist immer Ort vor Zeit (*place – time*).

355 ★★☆ Gibt es solche Schüler?

Setze die entsprechenden Adverbien der Häufigkeit ein.

They are loud (often). ______________________________

They run around (always). ______________________________

They have learned to sit still (never). ______________________________

They listen (never). ______________________________

They forget their homework (usually). ______________________________

Have you met such people (ever)? ______________________________

They drive their teachers crazy (sometimes). ______________________________

356 ★★☆ Adverbien der Art und Weise I

Übersetze folgende Sätze.

a) „Ich muss gehen", sagte er ruhig.

____

b) Er machte langsam die Tür zu.

____

c) Er schloss die Tür sorgfältig ab.

____

d) Dann öffnete er schnell seine Tasche.

____

e) Er steckte schnell den Schlüssel hinein.

____

355 They are often loud. They always run around. They have never learned to sit still. They never listen. They usually forget their homework. Have you ever met such people? Sometimes they drive their teachers crazy. / They sometimes drive their teachers crazy.
356 a) „I have to go", he said quietly. **b)** He slowly closed the door. / He closed the door slowly. **c)** He carefully locked the door. / He locked the door carefully. **d)** Then he quickly opened his bag. / Then he opened his bag quickly. **e)** He quickly put the key in it. / He put the key in it quickly.

357 ★★☆ Adverbien der Art und Weise II

Wo stehen Adverbien der Art und Weise? Sieh dir den Kurztest 356 an, dann weißt du es wieder.

1. In Sätzen ohne Objekt stehen die Adverbien der Art und Weise

   - vor dem Verb
   - nach dem Verb

2. In Sätzen mit einem Objekt stehen die Adverbien

   - vor dem Verb
   - am Satzende

3. Sie stehen jedoch nie zwischen dem ________________ und dem ________________.

358 ★★☆ Was für eine Klasse!

Bilde Sätze mit den folgenden Angaben. Setze das Adverb an die richtige Stelle.

Pupils in this class …

(loudly) never shout ________________________________.

(quietly) work ________________________________.

(quickly) do their homework ________________________________.

(politely) listen to their teacher ________________________________.

(correctly) answer questions ________________________________.

(noisily) don't run around ________________________________.

(carefully) word* their sentences ________________________________.

(nervously) don't act ________________________________.

(too hard) don't work ________________________________.

(impolitely) don't behave** ________________________________.

* to word something = etwas formulieren

** to behave = sich verhalten

357 1. nach dem Verb; **2.** vor dem Verb, am Satzende; **3.** nie zwischen dem Verb und dem Objekt.
358 Pupils in this class … never shout loudly / work quietly / do their homework quickly / listen to their teachers politely / answer questions correctly / don't run around noisily / word their sentences carefully / don't act nervously / don't work too hard / don't behave impolitely.

359 ★★☆ Eine Geschichte

a) Lies diese Geschichte und unterstreiche die Konjunktionen, die du in diesem Text findest.

A man and his dog are walking along a road. Suddenly the man remembers that he and his dog are already dead. He stops for a moment, but then walks on. After some time they come to a high, white wall. When they get near it, they see a big door in the wall and realize that the street which leads into it is made of pure gold. Then they see a man who is standing there. When they get near enough, they ask him where they are. The man tells them that this place is called heaven.

b) Welche Aufgaben haben die Konjunktionen in diesem Text?

____

____

360 ★★☆ Eine kleine Liste

a) Was bedeuten diese Konjunktionen auf Deutsch?

and	____________	if	________ / ________
or	____________	when	____________
but	____________	that	____________
so	____________	so that	____________
		because	____________
		although	____________
		before	____________
		until	____________

b) Was verbinden Konjunktionen wie *and*? Was verbinden Konjunktionen wie *if*?

____

359 a) A man and his dog are walking along a road. Suddenly the man remembers that he and his dog are already dead. He stops for a moment, but then he walks on. After some time they come to a high, white wall. When they get near it, they see a big door in the wall and realize that the street which leads into it is made of pure gold. Then they see a man who is standing there. When they get near enough, they ask him where they are. The man tells them that this place is called heaven. **b)** Sie verbinden gleiche Satzteile (z.B. zwei Substantive) oder einen Haupt- mit einem Nebensatz.

360 a) *and* = und; *or* = oder; *but* = aber; *so* = so; *if* = wenn, falls/ob; *when* = wenn; *that* = dass; *so that* = so dass; *because* = weil; *although* = obwohl; *before* = bevor; *until* = bis **b)** Konjunktionen wie *and, or, but, so* verbinden gleiche Satzteile (z.B. zwei Substantive) oder gleiche Satzarten (z.B. zwei Hauptsätze), Konjunktionen wie *if, when* dagegen verbinden Hauptsätze mit Nebensätzen.

361 ★★☆ Hausaufgaben

Kreuze die Konjunktionen an, die diesen Sätzen einen Sinn geben. Manchmal gibt es mehr als nur eine richtige Antwort.

a) I couldn't do my homework yesterday evening ____________ I was so tired.

- because
- if
- until
- before

b) I couldn't do my homework yesterday ____________ I got home.

- because
- if
- until
- before

c) I did my homework ____________ it was very difficult.

- before
- when
- although
- until

d) I did my homework ____________ I got home.

- before
- when
- although
- until

e) I'll do my homework ____________ I go to bed.

- when
- if
- because
- before

f) I'll do my homework ____________ I have time.

- when
- if
- because
- before

362 ★★☆ Die Fortsetzung …

Übersetze die Konjunktionen und setze sie richtig ein.

____________ (als) the man hears that he is in heaven, he is very surprised. It's such a wonderful place. Then he remembers that he ____________ (und) his dog are very thirsty. "Can I have some water, sir?" he asks the man. The man tells him ____________ (dass) he can have as much water as he wants, ____________ (aber) that dogs aren't allowed to come in. ____________ (wenn) he hears this, he is surprised again. He wants to go in, ____________ (aber) he decides to walk on.

361 a) because; **b)** until, before; **c)** although; **d)** before, when; **e)** before; **f)** when, if.
362 When (als); and (und); that (dass); but (aber); When (wenn); but (aber)

363 ★★★ ...und das Ende

Setze die folgenden Konjunktionen ein:

until *and* *so* *when* *that* *then* *because* *if*

After a long walk they come to another building with a big door in it. ______ they come near it, they see a man again. The man with the dog asks him ______ they can have some water. "Sure," the man answers, "There is enough water for everybody, also for your dog." ______ they go in ______ drink ______ they are full. ______ the man with the dog asks the other man: "What do you call this place?" "Well, this place is heaven." "Well, this is strange ______ the other man down the road called his place heaven, too." "Oh, you mean that place with the golden street? No, that's hell." "Doesn't it make you angry ______ they call their place heaven, too?" "No, it doesn't. We are happy ______ they help us find out which people leave their best friends behind for a little bit of water."

364 ★★★ Dein Urteil

Vervollständige diese Sätze, indem du die richtigen Konjunktionen einsetzt.

a) I didn't know ______ people could be so cruel.

b) I liked the story ______ it was short and interesting.

c) I didn't understand the story ______ you explained it to me.

d) I didn't understand it ______ I read it for the first time!

e) I can't believe ______ some people leave their best friends behind for a little bit of water.

363 When / if / So / and / until / Then / because / when oder that / that oder because
364 a) that; **b)** because; **c)** until, before; **d)** when; **e)** that.

365 ★☆☆ Was sie so tun

Definiere die hervorgehobenen Substantive. Verwende ein Relativpronomen.

a bus driver / drive a bus

Beispiel: A bus driver is somebody ______________________.

a shopkeer / have got a shop

______________________.

a shop assistant / work in a shop

______________________.

a customer / buy things in a shop

______________________.

an apprentice* / to learn a trade**

______________________.

* apprentice = Lehrling
** trade = Handwerk, Beruf; Handel

366 ★★☆ *Who* oder *which?*

Bilde Sätze mit *which* und *who*.

1) A teacher is somebody ______________ asks a lot of questions.
2) A classmate is somebody ______________ is in the same class.
3) School is something ______________ is never boring.
4) A school report is something ______________ can make my parents cry.
5) A pupil is somebody ______________ still goes to school.
6) Homework is something ______________ can drive you crazy.
7) An English lesson is something ______________ can be fun.

365 A bus driver is somebody who drives a bus. A shop keeper is somebody who has got a shop. A shop assistant is somebody who works in a shop. A customer is somebody who buys things in a shop. An apprentice is somebody who learns a trade.

366 1) who; **2)** who; **3)** which; **4)** which; **5)** who; **6)** which; **7)** which.

367 ★★☆ Ein Mädchen

Setze *who, which* oder *whose* ein.

a) Do you remember the girl ______________ photo I showed you yesterday?

b) That's the girl ______________ father is a teacher.

c) Yesterday she was in the bus ______________ stops near our house.

d) She was reading the book ______________ we talked about yesterday.

e) She's somebody ______________ can really drive you crazy.

f) She's a girl ______________ thinks she knows everything.

g) She is somebody ______________ thinks that she is more intelligent than others.

h) That's something ______________ is very difficult for me to understand.

368 ★★☆ Debbie and Tom

Setze die Relativpronomen nur dann ein, wenn du sie einsetzen musst.

a) Do you know the photo ______________ I gave to John? The one over there?

b) That's a photo of Debbie. You know? The girl ______________ Tom likes so much?

c) She lives in a place ______________ isn't very far from his street.

d) She is the most intelligent girl ______________ he knows.

e) That's the girl ______________ maths tests are better than his.

f) She's good at sports, too. Hockey is the game ______________ she is best at.

g) And she's good-looking. Tom thinks she is the most beautiful girl ______________ he has ever seen.

367 a) whose; **b)** whose; **c)** which; **d)** which; **e)** who; **f)** who; **g)** who; **h)** which.
368 a) –; **b)** –; **c)** which; **d)** –; **e)** whose; **f)** –; **g)** –

369 ★★☆ Eine Liebesgeschichte ...

Verbinde beide Sätze. Ein Hauptsatz wird dabei zu einem Relativsatz!

Debbie is **the girl**. Tom is in love with **her**.

____

Debbie is **the girl**. He is interested in **her**.

____

Debbie is **the girl**. He dreams of **her**.

____

Tom is **the boy**. Debbie is looking for **him**.

____

370 ★★☆ Welcher Film war es?

Bilde Relativsätze. Lasse das Relativpronomen aus, wenn es nicht notwendig ist.

Do you know the film? It's on TV tonight.

____

Do you know the actor? He plays the main character* in it.

____

Didn't Richard Gere play a part in the film? You saw it some days ago.

____

What was the title of the film? He was in the film.

____

Didn't you see it with Debbie? You know the girl. She is Tom's friend.

____

* main character = Hauptfigur

369 Debbie is the girl Tom is in love with. Debbie is the girl he is interested in. Debbie is the girl he dreams of. Tom is the boy she is looking for.
370 Do you know the film which is on TV tonight? Do you know the actor who plays the main character in it? Didn't Richard Gere play a part in the film you saw some days ago? What was the title of the film he was in? Didn't you see it with Debbie? You know the girl who is Tom's friend.

371 ★★☆ Was du wissen solltest …

Kreuze an, was richtig ist.

1. Relativsätze beziehen sich immer auf ○ a) ein Substantiv ○ b) ein Verb
2. Sie stehen daher ○ a) unmittelbar nach ○ b) unmittelbar vor

   dem jeweiligen Wort, auf das sie sich beziehen.
3. Relativsätze werden durch ein Relativpronomen eingeleitet. Die entsprechenden Relativpronomen sind *who, which, whose.*

   Who bezieht sich ○ a) auf Sachen ○ b) auf Personen

   Which bezieht sich ○ a) auf Sachen ○ b) auf Personen

   Whose bezieht sich ○ a) auf beides ○ b) nur auf Personen
4. *Who* und *which* können nicht ausgelassen werden, wenn sie

   ○ a) Objekt ○ b) Subjekt des Relativsatzes sind.

372 ★★☆ Ein letzter Versuch …

Verbinde beide Hauptsätze miteinander. Lasse das Relativpronomen weg, wo es nicht notwendig ist.

What did you do with the money? I gave it to you yesterday.

____?

I bought the book. You were looking for the book.

____.

Is that the book? We were talking about it.

____?

What's the name of the author? He wrote that book.

____?

371 1 a); **2** a); **3** who – b), which – a), whose – a); **4** b)

372 What did you do with the money I gave to you yesterday? I bought the book you were looking for. Is that the book we were talking about? What's the name of the author who wrote that book?

373 ★☆☆ Tom sagt, dass …

Setze die folgenden Sätze in die indirekte Rede.

Tom says:

"I can't come." ______________________________.

"I haven't done my homework yet." ______________________________.

"I've got no time." ______________________________.

"I have to help my mother." ______________________________.

"We must do some shopping." ______________________________.

"We will be back in the late afternoon." ______________________________.

"You can ring me up then." ______________________________.

"I won't go out again." ______________________________.

374 ★★☆ Was du wissen solltest …

Was ändert sich, was nicht? Ergänze bitte, was fehlt.

a) Was in der direkten Rede steht, wird zu einem: ● 1) Nebensatz ● 2) Hauptsatz

b) Dem Nebensatz geht ein Hauptsatz voraus, der ein einleitendes

● 1) Verb ● 2) Substantiv enthält.

c) Der Nebensatz wird mit ● 1) *than* ● 2) *that* eingeleitet, was auch entfallen kann.

d) Die Zeiten im Nebensatz ändern sich ● 1) nicht ● 2) immer ● 3) oft.

e) Im Nebensatz ändern sich die

● 1) Adjektive ● 2) Substantive ● 3) Pronomen und die Verbformen.

Sie werden der Sicht des Sprechers angepasst.

373 Tom says that he can't come. He says that he hasn't done his homework yet. He says that he has got no time. He says that he has to help his mother. He says that they must do some shopping. He says that they will be back in the late afternoon. He says that he / she can ring him up then. He says that he won't go out again.

374 a) 1) Nebensatz; **b)** 1) Verb; **c)** 2) *that*; **d)** 1) nicht; **e)** 3) Pronomen und die Verbformen

375 ★★☆ Ein Telefongespräch

Setze die folgenden Sätze in die indirekte Rede, nimm aber nicht immer das gleiche einleitende Verb. Möglich sind hier:

to say (to sb), to explain (to sb), to believe, to be sure, to think, to add, to shout, to answer, to know, to write

Debbie:

"I'm ill." ______________________________.

"I have to stay in bed." ______________________________.

"I've got the flu." ______________________________.

"Mum called a doctor." ______________________________.

Tom:

"I'm very sorry." ______________________________.

"I hope you will feel better soon." ______________________________.

"I'll tell Mr Mason that you're ill." ______________________________.

376 ★★☆ Am nächsten Tag

Setze die folgenden Sätze in die indirekte Rede.

Tom asks / wants to know:

"Do you feel better today?" ______________________________.

"Can you get up?" ______________________________.

"Did the doctor come?" ______________________________.

"Do you have to stay in bed?" ______________________________.

"Can I come to see you?" ______________________________.

"Have you taken any medicine?" ______________________________.

375 Debbie says that she is ill. She explains that she has got the flu. She adds that her mum called a doctor. Tom answers that he is very sorry. He says that he hopes that she doesn't feel very bad. He thinks / is sure / believes that she will feel better soon. He adds that he will tell Mr Mason that she is ill.

376 Tom asks Debbie if she feels better today. He wants to know if she can get up. Then he asks her if the doctor came. He wants to know if she has to stay in bed. He also wants to know if he can come to see her. Then he asks her if she has taken any medicine.

377 ★★☆ Was du vielleicht noch weißt ...

Kreuze an, was richtig ist.

1. Um was für Satztypen handelt es sich in dem vorigen Kurztest?

   ● a) Fragen ● b) Aussagesätze

2. Welche einleitenden Verben musst du gebrauchen?

   ● a) *to say* ● b) *to ask* ● c) *to want to know*

3. Welche Konjunktion musst du dann gebrauchen?

   ● a) *that* ● b) *if*

4. Wie sieht es mit der Wortstellung im Nebensatz aus? Musst du dieselbe Wortstellung

   ● a) wie in der Frage ● b) wie im Aussagesatz (SPO) gebrauchen?

5. Musst du im indirekten Fragesatz die *to do*-Umschreibung gebrauchen?

   ● a) ja ● b) nein

6. Muss am Satzende ein Fragezeichen stehen?

   ● a) ja ● b) nein

378 ★★☆ Auf ein Neues ...

Setze in die indirekte Rede.

Debbie's mother asks / wants to know *(in a conversation with the doctor)*:

"Can her friends visit her?" ______________________.

"Is she very ill?" ______________________.

"Has she got the flu?" ______________________.

"Does she feel very bad?" ______________________.

"Does she have a temperature?" ______________________.

"Will she get better soon?" ______________________.

377 1 a) Fragen; **2** b) to ask / c) to want to know; **3** b) if; **4** b) wie im Aussagesatz; **5** b) nein; **6** b) nein.
378 Her mother wants to know if her friends can visit her. She asks the doctor if she is very ill. She wants to know if she has got the flu. She wants to know if she feels very bad. She asks if she has a temperature. She asks him if she will get better soon.

379 ★★☆ Debbie ist zurück

Setze die Sätze in die indirekte Rede.

Her friends ask her / want to know:

"How long were you ill?" ______________________.

"What did you have?" ______________________.

"When could you get up again?" ______________________.

"Why weren't you here last week?" ______________________.

"What did you do all day?" ______________________.

"Who came to see you?" ______________________.

380 ★★★ Und was die Lehrer sagen

Setze die Sätze in die indirekte Rede. Pass auf das einleitende Verb auf!

Debbie's teachers say to her when she gets back:

"It's nice to see you again." ______________________.

"Are you feeling better?" ______________________.

"What did you have, Debbie?" ______________________.

"Do you feel better now?" ______________________.

"Do you know what we are doing now?" ______________________.

"Did anybody bring you your homework?" ______________________.

"Could you do any homework?" ______________________.

"Were you really ill?" ______________________.

"You missed a test." ______________________.

379 Her friends ask her / want to know: how long she was ill / what she had / when she could get up again / why she wasn't here last week / what she did all day / who came to see her.

380 One teacher says that it's nice to see her again. Another one asks if she's feeling better. A third teacher asks what she had. Another one wants to know if she feels better. One teacher asks her if she knows what they're doing now. Another teacher asks if anybody brought her her homework. Another teacher asks her if she could do any homework. A fourth teacher asks if she was really ill. Another one says that she missed a test.